23275

DATE DUE

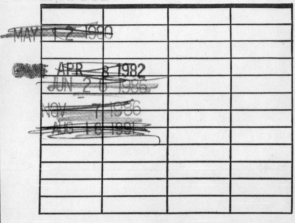

~~MAY 1 2 1990~~			
~~APR 8 1982~~			
~~JUN 2 0 1986~~			
~~NOV 1 1986~~			
~~AUG 1 6 1991~~			

P

Patterns
In
Human
Interaction

~~~~~~

An Introduction
To
Clinical Sociology

PATTERNS IN HUMAN INTERACTION

Henry L. Lennard

Arnold Bernstein

Jossey-Bass Inc., Publishers
615 Montgomery Street • San Francisco • 1969

PATTERNS IN HUMAN INTERACTION
An Introduction to Clinical Sociology
by Henry L. Lennard and Arnold Bernstein

Jossey-Bass, Inc., Publishers
615 Montgomery Street
San Francisco, California 94111

Library of Congress Catalog Card Number 70-75935

Standard Book Number SBN 87589-032-6

Printed in the United States of America
by York Composition Company, Inc., York, Pennsylvania
Bound by Chas. H. Bohn & Co., Inc., New York, New York
Jacket design by Willi Baum, San Francisco

FIRST EDITION

6902

THE JOSSEY-BASS BEHAVIORAL SCIENCE SERIES

General Editors

WILLIAM E. HENRY, *University of Chicago*

NEVITT SANFORD, *Stanford University and Wright Institute, Berkeley*

The Twentieth Century may well take its place in history as that century in which an understanding of communicational process began to be the central topic of intellectual interest.

Harley C. Shands

Preface

"I am a part of all that
I have met," says Tennyson's Ulysses at the close of his journeys.
At the end of our journey into the territory of human interaction
theory, we acknowledge the colleagues and friends whose ideas have
become a part of us.

We were very fortunate to have been able to learn from our
friends Donald D. Jackson, Daniel R. Miller, Harley C. Shands,
Norman W. Bell, Edward Rose, Marie Coleman Nelson, and David
R. Kessler. The influence of Robert F. Bales, Gregory Bateson, Robert F. Merton, and Jurgen Ruesch on our work will be apparent to
anyone familiar with their work.

Supportive administrative settings were provided at Columbia University by Allen H. Barton and Clara Shapiro and subsequently by Leon Epstein and Alexander Simon at the Langley-Porter Neuropsychiatric Institute and the San Francisco Medical Center of the University of California. We are most appreciative of their encouragement.

Our research assistants and students, Nolan G. Embrey at Columbia University, Donald C. Ransom and Carol L. Huffine at the University of California, and Maria Mayser at the University of Cologne, provided valuable help in the studies reported here.

In the collection of data on patients and families, helpful cooperation was extended by Nathan S. Kline and Lawrence C. Kolb.

Our research was supported by a research grant from the National Institute of Mental Health and by a Career Scientist Award (K-3MH 18,697) to one of us (Lennard). We are most grateful to the National Institute, to members of the study sections, and to its administrative staff, most especially to Bert E. Boothe, chief of the Research Fellowships Section, for support and confidence in our efforts.

San Francisco   HENRY L. LENNARD
New York   ARNOLD BERNSTEIN
  January, 1969

Contents

7   Functions of Human Interaction   174
      Therapeutic Interaction • *System Properties
      of Interaction Processes* • *Deutero-Learning
      • Interaction as End in Itself*

Patterns
In
Human
Interaction

An Introduction
To
Clinical Sociology

Introduction

Clinical Sociology: A New Focus

This book is about theory and research in the study of human interaction. In it, we have undertaken to explore and explicate how individuals may be shaped and transformed through their participation in human interactional contexts. The questions that we consider are not exclusively the subject matter of any single behavioral science discipline, though perhaps they are more closely related to the field of sociology than to any of the others.

The theme of the book revolves around the relation of social contexts to the interactional behaviors that occur within them. That social contexts do modify and influence human behavior, though not a novel proposition, deserves considerably more amplification than it has already received. Our book specifically undertakes to explore many of the ramifications of this hypothesis. Some of the questions that we shall consider are:

1. What are the different conceptions of social context?
2. What properties do social systems have in common?
3. How do the interactional processes in one social context differ from the interactional processes in another? For example, how does interaction in a psychotherapy context differ from interaction in a family context? How does interaction in a "disturbed" family differ from interaction in a "normal" family? How does interaction in a social system with a "psychotic" member differ from interaction in a social system with a "neurotic" member?
4. What properties of social contexts are "therapeutic" and what properties are "pathogenic"?
5. How can interaction be conceived of in process and developmental terms? How can operational measures based upon these conceptualizations be constructed?

The answers to these questions (all of which bear upon the relations between social contexts and social interaction) have considerable theoretical as well as practical consequences. The crucial issue to which our investigation addresses itself revolves around the extent to which interactional behavior is context-derived and context-contingent, and the extent to which it is a function of enduring individual and personality attributes. To what extent is human behavior generated by the social contexts in which it occurs and to what extent do individuals create a "portable" reality that determines their behavior, irrespective of the situation in which they find themselves?

The importance of ascertaining the relationship between social context and interactional behavior takes on added significance when questions arise concerning the nature, cause and cure of so-called deviant behavior, psychological impairment, and psychiatric symptomatology. For the proper elucidation of these problems demands an assessment of the extent to which deviance, mental illness, and symptomatology are characteristics of individuals or are immanent in contexts. This matter is not of theoretical interest alone but of the greatest possible practical importance, for whether a particular pathology is conceived to inhere in an individual or in a situation determines the locus and mode of the attempted inter-ventions. Psychotherapeutic intervention has traditionally located pathology within the individual and has focused its attention on the management of intrapsychic variables. In this book we shift the perspective from the individual and his intrapsychic states to the interactional environment within which his behavior is inevitably embedded. By so doing we shift the locus of the search for pa-thology from the individual to his interactional context, and thus open another arena for therapeutic intervention and investigation.

Of necessity, an inquiry into the nature of human interaction requires an approach from a variety of perspectives. We have uti-lized concepts from the behavioral sciences, systems theory, infor-mation theory, biology, psychiatry, and psychoanalysis as they seemed relevant.

We found it necessary and productive to combine social re-search methodology with clinical approaches. This application of social research methodology and sociological theory to the data of the "clinical" situation and to subject matter traditionally falling within the fields of psychiatry and clinical psychology seemed to us to deserve a new characterization, to which the term *clinical soci-ology* seems ideally suited.*

Our book represents a report on research in progress and theory in the making. The data, though rich by comparison to what has heretofore been available, are admittedly sparse when compared to what is required. Though our hypotheses are tentative, we be-lieve them to represent fertile sources of research potential. They will of course require revision as new data are collected. Our meth-odological proposals seem to us to be demanded by the requirements of the subject matter itself. Perhaps better methods will emerge as more conceptual leverage is acquired on what has until now re-mained a largely untapped and unexplored area for scientific ex-ploration.

The actual data and analysis in our studies focus mainly

* The term *clinical sociology* appears to have been introduced by Louis Wirth (1931) in a sense quite analogous to that proposed here. Among contemporary sociologists who have referred to clinical sociology is Gouldner (1965).

upon two kinds of human interaction contexts: families and psychotherapy dyads. The powerful influence that the family context exercises upon developmental processes among the individuals that make it up can hardly be doubted. A major influencing role has also been attributed to the psychotherapy context. But whether human groups or contexts identified by the rubric *psychotherapy* necessarily generate changes in behavior, or more significantly, changes that could be regarded as "therapeutic," is a question that bears scrutiny.

We collected and studied interactional protocols from different groups of families, one group that we treat as "control" families and one group that we treat as "disturbed" families. The so-called normal families are those in which no member has been identified as a patient. We also collected data from psychotherapy dyads, some including hospitalized schizophrenic patients and others composed of psychoneurotic patients seen in office practice.

The justification for the parallel study of family and therapy contexts arises from the premise that these two types of systems bear a special relation to each other. The same concepts and methods that apply to the description of therapy systems are also useful for the description of interaction in family systems, because both types of systems or contexts are actually subclasses of the more general category, human interaction systems. Therapy contexts are possibly able to induce changes in individuals by virtue of the same principles and processes that operate in family systems.

Though therapy groups are special social systems, the study of such systems allows access to behavioral data obtaining in a social relationship that extends over a period of time. For sociological theorists like Talcott Parsons, therapy represents a social control and socialization context involving sequences of behavior that are not too dissimilar from the processes of socialization and social control that take place within the family. For theoretically minded psychiatrists like Jerome Frank, psychotherapy belongs to a category of social situations that involve influence and planned change, ranging from religion to brainwashing.

The incorporation of psychotherapy into a framework that embraces the study of socialization, thought control, and social influence, as proposed by some sociologists and psychiatrists, results from the similarity of therapeutic interaction process to the processes of socialization as they occur in the family, the school, and other social settings. The study of the principles and processes operating in these social contexts constitutes the subject matter of what we have already referred to as *clinical sociology*.

PART ONE

NOTES ON
THEORY

~~~~~~

I*n Part One, the theoretical issues and conceptions related to the study of ongoing behavior processes are outlined. We first explicate two main conceptions, context and system, as they apply to interaction study. We then move on to very general theoretical conceptions of interaction. These conceptions are of major importance in the analysis and discussion of the data collected on family and therapy contexts. Then various methodological issues that are encountered in the study of interaction and change are presented. In Part Two, the orientations to the study of interaction processes previously introduced are applied in the examination of family and therapy contexts.*

Chapter 1

Interaction Process as Context and System

∿∿∿∿∿∿∿∿∿∿∿∿∿∿∿∿∿∿∿

Social scientists, despite their devotion to the study of behavior systems, have largely focused their attention only on the characteristics of the behavior that takes place within such systems rather than upon the characteristics of the systems themselves. Investigations into the properties of social systems are therefore scarce. Until recently, little work has been forthcoming about the relationships that obtain among the behavioral parameters of the system; about the configurations and sequences of behavior that are typical of different stages in the life of a system (for example, differences in behavior and expectations between early and later stages of friendship, work, family, and therapy systems); about the mechanisms for maintaining and regulating behavior processes and for reducing behavioral disparities; or about the relation of antecedent system states to subsequent outcomes.

SYSTEM PROPERTIES OF SOCIAL SYSTEMS

It is our intention to focus upon the social system, or the context in which social behavior takes place, and to elucidate some of its properties—those properties that affect the behaviors of the participants. We see social systems as a subclass of systems in general; as such, they are subject to the principles of general systems theory:

> General systems theory contends that there are principles of systems in general or in defined subclasses of systems irrespective of the nature of systems, of their components, or of the relations or "forces" between them (Bertalanffy, 1966, p. 708).

To set the stage for the analysis of the family and therapy data that we have collected, we shall offer a brief description of system properties of social systems that we consider to be significant for understanding factors related to disturbance (and restoration) in social interaction systems.

EQUILIBRIUM PROCESSES AND HOMEOSTASIS

The principle of homeostasis has to do with the permissible range of variation that may occur among the variables constituting a system, so that the system still retains its identity. Although the concept derives originally from the field of physiology, it seems basic for understanding certain social and communicational processes that occur in families and other interaction systems, such as psychotherapy. The maintenance of homeostasis requires an "ensemble of regulations that maintain variables constant and direct the organism toward a goal (Bertalanffy, 1966, p. 708)."

One property of any system is interdependence or order in the relationships among its components. Biological and social systems exhibit tendencies toward equilibrium (homeostasis). These homeostatic tendencies are processes within the system wherein some definite, definable order among the component parts is maintained such that the variables in the system range between specifiable limits. The tendency toward homeostasis in a system is revealed through the stability of a system or of the variables within a system.

The traditional example of physiological homeostasis is the tendency of the temperature of the human body to vary, for most of us, around a mean of 98.6 degrees Fahrenheit, irrespective of the external temperature. Normal homeostasis may be disturbed by insults to the body through bacterial invasion or environmental stress. A breakdown of a body's homeostatic controls is revealed by the failure of a body to maintain its temperature within permissible limits, and this in turn results in a disturbance of system function or even the death and disintegration of the system. Our hypothesis is that social systems in which homeostatic controls fail suffer the same fate.

One indicator of homeostasis is the stability of given parameters of a system when these parameters are observed at different points in time. Thus, for instance, system A would be more homeostatic than system B if the deviations in the means of given parameters of system A assessed at intervals in the life of the system were less than those of system B for comparable intervals. The work of Bales (1950), Chapple and Arensberg (1940), Matarazzo (1962), and our own (1960) have shown that though the distribution of participation varies for different social systems and their objectives and conditions, each system tends toward stability in the rate and volume of participation.

In our previous research on psychotherapy systems (1960), we analyzed the behavior of therapists and patients along a number of dimensions, both of a quantitative sort (for example, number of verbal propositions) and of a qualitative sort (for example, affective, evaluative, or descriptive). We found that there was a tendency for each therapist-patient dyad to establish a ratio between them for given types of participation around which they then tended to vary within rather narrow limits. Thus, we might note that the participants in one therapist-patient system, for example, maintained an interaction rate averaging two interactions per unit of time, while another pair might maintain an average interaction rate of about ten interactions per unit of time. Were homeostasis operating with respect to this parameter (that is, interaction rate), one would expect that interaction rates for each of these therapy systems would fluctuate around these means from session to session. We found that therapist-patient pairs do tend to establish an interaction rate "norm" by the second month of therapy, from which they then tend to vary very little.

The analytic value of the concept of homeostasis, as the physiologist, Emerson (1960), has quite correctly observed, lies in the possibilities it offers for quantitative ". . . comparisons between phenomena, that without it, are very hard to compare, because we don't have a quantitative relationship in quantitative terms that is applicable to the different phenomena (p. 243)."

For example, using our criterion for comparing the degree of homeostasis in different systems, that is, the deviations in the means of given parameters, one could compare the degree of homeostasis in different therapy systems by observing which therapist-patient pair shows least fluctuation for a given parameter from session to session, which shows the most; whether different treatment pairs in which the same therapist participates show the same or different degrees of stability; whether comparisons over time of the variations in the parameters of the same system vary from phase to phase; and whether there is systematic longitudinal development of the homeostatic properties of given social systems that are characteristic.

Besides communicative acts, a number of other parameters of various social systems come to mind. These parameters also lend themselves to unitization that can be quantified, and their interdependence and variation can be compared. One such qualitative parameter is the set of expectations of the participants in a system and the relationship between such expectations, as for instance, the expectations held by a husband and his wife. In marital relationships some expectations are mutual and complementary and others are not; some expectations are fulfilled, while others are not. The ratio of expectations met to those that are unmet differs from marriage to marriage. It might be argued that some marriages are more "stable" or more homeostatic than others (for better or for worse), insofar as the ratio of met to unmet expectations is constant or fluctuating. One would also expect that it should be possible to identify the processes within marital systems that are aimed at restoring the expectational balances around which the system normally remains stabilized.

When something "goes wrong" in a social interaction system, it results in a disequilibrium or strain in the system that either one or both of the participants may perceive. To preserve a system and to eliminate strain, processes must be set into motion to reduce it. For example, if one were engaged in a conversation with somebody who suddenly became mute and discontinued the conversation, one might have, among other things, to reexamine the conversational sequences to discover what had gone wrong. One might discover that he had said something to offend the other person, and if he wanted to reestablish effective communication, he would have to take the necessary reparative steps to coax or induce the partner to resume the conversation. Both partners in a social system are important vectors in maintaining that system, but deficiencies in one can be compensated by the other, and the progression of interaction can be maintained.

In order for interaction systems to move forward to the accomplishment of their objectives, they apparently require a minimum level of exchange of certain kinds of specific communication. Each member of an interactional system makes a contribution to the system. Each is a source of intrasystem input. Though different kinds of systems may vary as to the specific amount of intrasystem input required to maintain the system, most systems cannot continue to exist without specifiable minimum inputs from the participants. These intrasystem behavioral inputs seem to be of two kinds: (1) informational (orienting and socializing communications); and (2) emotional or affective. Any or all of the participants in a social system must provide the required minimum level of these two basic kinds of inputs in order for a social system to survive. It is not necessarily the case that each system member must contribute an equal amount of the required informational and emotional input but rather that when deficits in such behaviors occur on the part of certain system members, they must be compensated for by other system members. Social systems may fail as readily because of the failure on the part of some members to increase their contributions as they do because of the failure on the part of some members to maintain theirs.

Different kinds of social systems are characterized by different expected ratios of intrasystem input among the participants. Failure to maintain such ratios may be disruptive to the system as well as to the individual participants in the system. There is ample evidence, for instance, that deficits in cognitive and emotional inputs among family members have disruptive effects on both the family as a system and the members of the family as individuals.

LONGITUDINAL PROCESSES

Just as different systems may be measured against the criterion of stability, so might a single system be compared with itself at different points in time. The concept of stability is itself a time function. It assumes the persistence of a process over time, and comparisons with respect to stability require equal time intervals. If one wanted to gain a longitudinal perspective on the development of homeostatic processes in a social system of fairly long duration, one might want to observe the fluctuations of the parameters of that system throughout the duration of that system. It might be assumed that if the fluctuations of the interactional parameters of the system remain constant, the system is stable; if they increase, the system is becoming more unstable; and if the magnitude of the fluctuations decrease, homeostasis of the system is increasing.

To illustrate this idea, we constructed a theoretical curve of fluctuation in the magnitude of a set of variables over the duration of a hypothetical social system (*see* Figure 1). In our model, the fluctuation of the variable takes the form of a steadily decreasing oscillation around a system mean. This model represents only one

possible kind of curve that might be identified by studying changes
through time in system parameters. It was our impression, although
we did not have data through long enough time periods, that some
of the parameters in psychotherapy systems vary in this way.

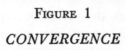

FIGURE 1

CONVERGENCE

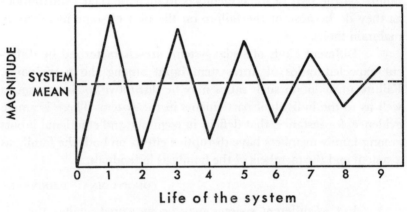

HYPOTHETICAL CURVE OF FLUCTUATION

CONVERGENCE

The curve illustrated in Figure 1 exhibits one form of a
system property that can be called *convergence*. Convergence is one
of the consequences that interaction in social systems may be expected to accomplish, because interaction between individuals tends
to decrease dissimilarities in their expectations, goals, and behavior.
Evidence is accumulating that the process of interaction results in
moving interactors not only toward more symmetrical orientations
(Newcomb, 1953) but also toward more similar patterns of communication (Lennard and Bernstein, 1960; Strupp, 1960; Pepinsky,
1964).

In many social systems, especially those involving socialization or acculturation (for example, family, therapy, education),
information about specific role relationships and their requirements
is unequally distributed among the participants in the system. Com-

munication, through interaction, reduces or eliminates these informational imbalances and equalizes the distribution of information among the participants in the interaction system. One way of reducing expectational dissimilarities is through inquiring and receiving information about what behavior and attitudes are appropriate to each of the role partners. Processes of informational exchange among the participants in a social system are essential for the establishment, maintenance, and development of the system.

PHASE, DIFFERENTIATION, AND SERIAL PROCESSES

Group and system theorists have used the concept of differentiation to denote certain kinds of sequential changes that characterize social interaction processes. The patterns and the kinds of behaviors that are contributed by members of a group appear to be contingent, in part, upon the period of time that the group has interacted. For example, individuals who know each other are more likely to discuss personal subjects than those who have met only once. Members of experimental problem-solving groups begin to make problem-solving suggestions only after they have had a period of orientation together to consider what the problem is.

The accomplishment of the purposes for which any group is formed requires different patterns of performances on the part of the group members during different phases of the process. For example, during the first phase of the formation of a theatrical group to put on a play, the group members would be engaged in play selection, casting, and planning. During the next phase they might be engaged in rehearsal and scenery construction, and during the final phase, they would engage in performances on the stage. The purposes and goals for which individuals interact in groups require a differentiation of action through time. Bertalanffy (1966) believes the principle of differentiation to be ubiquitous—in biology, the evolution and development of the nervous system, behavior, psychology, and culture.

Werner (1957) writes, "Wherever development occurs, it proceeds from a state of globality and lack of differentiation to a state of increasing differentiation, articulation and hierarchic order (p. 126)." Groups enter different phases of differentiation during

different stages in their development. The phase of development
or differentiation forms an important part of the context in which
group members interact at any given point in the group process.
Whenever systematic study of social systems extending over any
major period of time has been undertaken, such phase phenomena
have been observed. Observations appear to support the view that
there are changes in the content, focus, and direction of role relationships as the development of a group unfolds. For instance, psychotherapists and patients usually do not undertake to explore a
patient's feelings in depth until after the definition of the therapist-
patient role relationship has been established.

Despite the fact that contacts among the participants in a
role relationship are intermittent, behavior within the system is continuous. Members of a system, when they resume interaction after a
period of interruption, locate themselves in the same context and
phase within the relationship as before. In terms of the subject matter, emotional quality, and allocation of behavior, individuals tend
to resume where they left off.

Even quantitative data show continuity in the numerical
values of system parameters (frequencies of specific communicative
acts) from session to session. In our (1960) study of psychotherapy
systems involving neurotic patients, socializing and affective communications showed a consistent increase or decrease from session
to session, as if the participants had been informed of the proportion
of a certain kind of statements that they had contributed to the
preceding session. It might be noted that we did not find this type
of serial continuity to be so clear in social systems containing a
schizophrenic member.

EXTRASYSTEM INPUT AND ADAPTATION

Social systems are "open systems"; there is a continuous
flow and exchange across system boundaries. Social systems are
constantly exposed to extrasystem inputs, some of which impose a
stress upon the system. Continuous adjustments and new adaptations are required and must be accomplished by a social system to
accommodate this diversity of external influences that impinge upon
it. Just as the body's internal temperature regulatory system has to

adjust to extreme changes in environmental temperature, so must intrasystemic social interactive processes serve the purposes of adaptation in social systems.

External stress may act upon a social system through its effects either upon individual members of the system or upon the system as a whole. Father's irritability after a hard day's work would impose a system "load" of the former type, while geographical relocation of a family could be conceived of as an example of a system "load" of the latter type. Stresses or loads upon a therapy system can be conceptualized as taking the form of factors acting upon a patient or a therapist in their extratherapy system contacts, their daily life. Even a therapist's overconformity to a particular school of psychiatric thought might "stress" the system and impose the necessity for homeostatic readjustments in the therapist-patient interaction system (see Lennard and Bernstein, 1960).

One criterion for the adaptive capacity of a social system might be its ability to deal with extrasystem stresses through internal interactional and sequential modifications, without being disrupted.

Clinicians often refer to family adaptation or the failure of adaptation in a family interaction system when it is confronted with stressful external influences. Therapy systems, too, sometimes fail when they cannot adapt to the external forces acting upon them, such as interfering relatives or the patient's loss of income.

Ackerman (1958) notes the effect upon a family when a husband comes home feeling defeated by his day's battle in the occupational world. An adaptation to such an extrasystem load, communicated to the family by one of its members, may consist of an increase in compensatory intrafamily interactions, "supportive" interactions (mothering) by other family members.

Let us consider the effect upon a therapy system of the external stresses in a patient's life that, in an early phase of treatment, result in his arrival at his session crying and unable to talk. It would be expected that during this session many of the parameters of therapist-patient behavior would differ considerably from the means that had been previously established. Such fluctuations in the treatment parameters (for example, allocation of verbal behavior, amount of orienting communication) might reflect either the disruptive effect of external stress or the reparative and adjustive homeostatic mechanisms called into play by system maintenance processes.

Therapy systems that can minimize fluctuations in their parameters under stressful conditions should be considered the most homeostatic. The goal of adaptation in a social system could be formulated as the restoration of balanced interactional patterns.

We also assume that external stresses introduced into a therapy system at a later phase in therapy would not result in as great fluctuations in the treatment parameters as would stresses introduced at an earlier phase in therapy. Although at a later phase in treatment the patient might talk more about his distress, hence making the *content* of his talking in a later session different from that of an earlier session, we would not expect the *interaction process* to undergo as great an alteration. Nor would we expect that the configuration and sequences of communication between therapist and patient would depart quite so much from the pattern established in preceding sessions. Thus, the same environmental stress occurring late in therapy would not disequilibrate the therapist-patient interactional system as much as stress occurring early in therapy.

One reason for this stability is that the patient has become socialized to the therapy system and has been inducted into the patient role. One important component of this role, which he has learned, is that a patient is supposed to verbalize his feelings, ideas, and reactions. Thus, what was formerly an extrasystem input has now become grist for the therapeutic mill, and has been transformed into a functional intrasystem input.

We believe that role-learning and mutual socialization in social systems is analogous to the processes of growth, differentiation, and adaptation in biological systems; and that role-differentiation in social systems is equivalent to biological adaptation in biological systems.

CONTEXT AS MESSAGE

If social settings or social contexts do indeed modify and alter the patterning of interaction, then researchers in this area naturally must determine exactly what a social context is and how to define the difference between one social context and another; and they must determine what an interaction process is composed of and how to describe it. These problems pose many difficult and complex theoretical and methodological issues. One of the major theoretical obstacles, one with many methodological implications, is that the phrase *social context* incorporates a variety of meanings and refers to a variety of different situations. For the sake of clarification, and in order that the reader might anticipate the structure of our theoretical approach and research methodology, we will discuss the several senses in which *social context* is used in this book and some of the implications of the different meanings.

In traditional sociological theory, *social context* refers to *a complex of interrelated roles and statuses*. Within the framework of this meaning, a family and a psychotherapy group constitute different social contexts. An individual within a family is in a different social context than the same individual is when he is in a psychotherapy group. By implication, individuals are expected to behave (interact) differently in one social context than in the other.

But sociologists and anthropologists also define a social context according to a second set of criteria. Social groups composed of members *possessing the same social, educational, economic or cultural attributes* are said to constitute a social context. Thus, a middle-class Italian-American family would be classified as a different social context than a middle-class Protestant New England family. By implication, individuals belonging to one of these special contexts are expected to behave (interact) differently from individuals belonging to the other.

Some work (for example, the comparison of interaction processes in families with the interaction processes in psychotherapy) rests upon the first of these definitions, while some (for example, the comparison of German with American families) rests upon the second.

A third sense in which the phrase *social context* is employed is that of a social group containing members *possessing common psychological attributes*. This definition is implied by much of the work done in clinical settings or by clinicians, whenever an attempt to discriminate between interaction in "disturbed" and "healthy" families is undertaken. It rests upon the assumption that social contexts that contain "neurotic," "psychotic," or "normal" members are inherently different from one another, according to the psychological attributes of their members. Two of the main studies in clinical sociology that we report in this book were designed to explore some of the implications of this definition of social context. In one, families containing a "schizophrenic" child are compared with a group of control families. In the other psychotherapy dyads containing a "psychotic" are compared with those containing a "neurotic."

In the course of our research and conceptualizing there emerged a fourth way of looking at the problem of social context. We began to see that the traditional ways of looking at social contexts did not do justice to their system character and their interactional properties. The older classifications are based upon static and extrinsic variables rather than the dynamic and intrinsic properties of the contexts themselves. We realized that differences in social contexts might be seen as a function of what was actually happening within them interactionally. From this point of view a social context could be defined as consisting of the *configurations and sequences of interaction* obtaining in a social system, that is, an interactional environment. In this sense, social contexts are considered to be different only insofar as they are interactionally different. This fourth conceptualization of "social context" has some important implications.

Social process occurs within the medium of human interaction. This medium is more pervasive than any of the other media that influence human conduct. Though it is not often recognized, human interaction acts both as the context and the substance of significant human behavior. It is both a form of social technology and an environment within which social behavior takes place.

In his book, *Understanding Media,* Marshall McLuhan (1966) examines the role that various other media such as television, money, the printed word, and the movies play in effecting the very large changes in human outlook that are occurring in the world today. He observes that the introduction of any new technology gradually creates a new human environment. Such a new environment, he suggests, does not act just as a passive wrapping but as an active process that affects human behavior. The formative power in a medium is the medium itself. Every medium contains a message. The content of the message in any medium is always another medium. The content of writing is speech. The content of speech is thought. "The 'message' of any medium or technology is the change of scale or pace or pattern that it introduces into human affairs (p. 24)." Like McLuhan, we wish to consider some of "the psychic and social consequences of . . . designs or patterns as they amplify or accelerate existing [social] processes (p. 24)."

The designs and patterns to which we allude here are the interactional configurations and sequences that prevail in various specific social settings. Because they are primarily behavior-influencing contexts, we believe it to be especially important to study and define the *interactional configurations* that prevail in psychotherapy and in family settings.

Unfortunately, as McLuhan rightly observes, "the content of a medium is like the juicy piece of meat carried by the burglar to distract the watchdog of the mind (p. 32)." Effects of a medium that are unrelated to its content easily pass unnoticed even by the most sophisticated observers. "It's not what you do, but the way that you do it" is a homily that derives added significance from this perspective.

Consider, for example, the long-standing controversy about the effect of television on children. Although considerable speculation has revolved around the effect of program contents portraying violence and murder, hardly any discussion has focused on the possible effect of the medium itself—a medium that generates experiences that are turned on and off at will, that is regularly punctuated by irrelevancies (advertisements), and that requires arbitrary alteration between withdrawal and involvement. These are built-in characteristics of the medium itself, rather than of its content.

We are proposing a similar approach to the study of the influence of human interaction upon behavior. Rather than simply viewing the content of human interaction, we believe it to be at least equally important to view some of the effects of the formal and contextual properties of the interaction process itself. The configural properties of human interaction process contain messages, some of which may contradict or transcend the messages contained in the "content" of such interactions. For example, in a recent study of interaction patterns on a psychiatric ward in one therapeutic-community–oriented mental hospital, it was found that most nurse-patient contacts were less than one minute in duration (Longabaugh *et al.*, 1966). Consider the contradictory message that is transmitted to patients by such an abridged and atomistic interactional configuration when its message is compared to the explicit verbal commitment of the staff to the importance of human interaction for resocialization.

The interactional context of any interactional event is the larger situation or environment within which that event occurs. Any given interaction between persons is also part of an ongoing sequence of interactions; that sequence possesses formal configural properties of its own, independent of the content of the communications that compose the sequence. These sequential patterns constitute what we call an *interactional environment*. These patterns of interaction within social systems, such as the family or therapy, are often as significant as knowledge of the content is for understanding the behavior of individuals in those systems. Both the content and the context convey meaning.

Although many practicing clinicians, especially psychoanalysts, tend to focus their attention upon content rather than process variables when describing what transpires during psychotherapy, psychoanalytic practice itself does not preclude consideration of the importance of process variables. An interesting case in point is the problem of scheduling (frequency of visits, length of session, interruptions of treatment, and so on). Freud (1913) insisted, as many classical analysts still do, upon at least five visits a week. Glover (1955) went so far as to define any interval of more than forty-eight hours between visits as "an interruption" of the therapy process. Thus frequency of contacts or interval between contacts is regarded as being an important parameter of the treatment process. In their "flexible" approach, Alexander and French (1946) advocate utilization of changes in interval and frequency as part of the therapy process.

Scheduling is an example of a contentless attribute of a therapeutic setting. This "formal" contextual property of an interaction system is considered critical for the development of a patient's emotional involvement in therapy (transference reaction) and as a condition for the maintenance of a proper balance between therapy and the outside social settings in which the patient participates (to maintain "continuity of material").

In support of his contention that the central aspect of psychotherapy is in the content and meaning of what is said rather than in process variables, Wallerstein (1966), in a recent review of psychotherapy research, cites Colby's statement to the effect that "linguists and information theorists and now research psychotherapists avoid the essence of utterances. They shirk the fact that it is not statements themselves; it is the meaning and impact of statements that is crucial (p. 217)." To support this proposition, Wallerstein speculates that "one therapist may utter 200 sentences in a single session; another but one (after 40 minutes of silence) and have a far greater reverberative impact. Obviously so (p. 217)."

What Wallerstein implies is that the impact of a single meaningful statement can be far greater than that of many meaningless statements. But inadvertently the illustration lends itself equally well to a contextual explanation. A single utterance following forty minutes of silence constitutes a characteristic *configuration* of communication. A single communication following a long period of silence may very well exert an impact precisely *because* of its context and not in spite of it. So rather than underscoring the significance of meaning or content, which is the crux of Wallerstein's argument, his illustration very aptly supports the significance of context or communicational figure and ground relationships.

Fleming and Benedek (1966) emphasize process in psychoanalysis. They write, and this could well pertain to the illustration discussed above, "Like blips on a radar screen, specific phenomena . . . acquire more meaning when related to what they have come from and to what follows next (p. 54)."

The formal attributes of the interactional context and process within which therapy takes place must be studied further in order to learn to what extent they merely represent "prerequisites" to therapy and to what extent they are themselves a significant part of the "therapeutic message." Discussion must include not only "what" and "how" a patient "learns" in a therapy interaction, but also a description of its contextual properties. One attribute—for example, the experience of continuity—may be used to illustrate this approach.

In a sample of therapist-patient interactions involving a group of chronic schizophrenic patients, we observed that patients expressed more satisfaction with the sessions in which the therapist stayed on the same subject longer, irrespective of the depth or therapeutic significance of the subject under discussion. This kind of data suggests that the *experience* of taking part in an interactional configuration in which there is a continuous sequential interaction revolving around the same subject matter may take precedence over the significance of the *content* of the communication.

Similarly, our studies of family interaction show that family contexts generate communicational fields different from those generated by other social contexts, and that families with a schizophrenic member have particular communicational characteristics. But of most interest is the discovery that disturbed families differ from control families most significantly in sequential and process characteristics of interaction—in how interaction is distributed, directed, and programmed through time.

We believe that the effect of interactional context has not received the attention it deserves, despite an increasing concern with the relationship and system aspects of interaction, in part because of the difficulty of defining and quantifying the relevant segments of context to be studied. In order to understand what is communicated to an individual in a family or therapy setting, what messages he gets from his interactional environment, and what the effects are, one must find ways of characterizing the interactional configurations and sequences generated by and prevailing in social settings.

This effort is especially relevant to the study of clinical settings as they exist in hospitals, clinics, and other institutions. For if we can define the characteristics of an interactional field that are beneficial (facilitate changes in behavior, encourage new modes of interaction), it may be possible to create interactional environments that are not encumbered by institutional structures, but that fulfill the same function for individuals. Such configurations may be created more efficiently and less expensively than they presently are in so-called therapeutic settings.

Chapter 2

The Interactional Perspective

The social systems in which we have examined social action processes are psychotherapy dyads, families, and groups of families. Through the analysis of social process in such groups we have sought to identify interactional configurations and their effects and to learn how changes in the direction and focus of group action are determined. For the fullest understanding of how changes in the course of action processes in groups are fashioned, and especially how changes in interactional configurations are brought about, we found it necessary to assume a theoretical perspective broader than those represented by the two traditional theoretical orientations that are usually applied to the study of group behavior: sociology and psychology. The *sociological* perspective emphasizes situational and "system developmental" determinants of group process. The *psychological* perspective takes account of the personal and psychodynamic attributes of individual members of groups and of the role that given psychological events play in determining interactional configurations.

Those who adhere to a sociological perspective emphasize the influence of two sets of determinants upon behavior in social interaction. One set is described by the concepts of situation, setting, or context, or, more accurately, the social norms that govern particular situations, settings, or contexts. From this perspective social situations, settings, or contexts demand specific behavioral responses from persons within them. Individuals merely execute the performances and reactions that are assigned to them by the programs immanent in various social settings. Of somewhat more recent interest to sociologists is a second set of determinants, deriving from the *process* of social interaction itself. These determinants derive from a longitudinal view of social process and may be described as developmental or phase properties of social groups or systems. This view requires that in addition to observing the type of social setting (system) within which individuals are interacting, one needs to know *when* within the life of the system (what phase of developmental sequence) the interaction is taking place in order to understand or predict the behavior of individual actors.

Those who adhere to the psychological perspective tend to regard individual psychological attributes of group members as salient. For the most part, individuals are seen as behaving with a certain consistency irrespective of the situation or context and the phase of the system their action is located in. The advocates of this theoretical position allow for a range of behavioral variability as an individual engages in role-appropriate performances, but they rely mainly on personality variables or psychodynamics for predicting behavior.

The sociological perspective concerns itself with the properties of systems or contexts within which individuals interact and the effects such system variables have on the direction of the behavior of individuals in a group. Application of this approach to any particular group for the purpose of predicting the course of action in that group requires an assumption that the group belongs to a particular class of groups operating under similar conditions. Groups of a similar class are expected to manifest characteristic distributions in given parameters of action. Thus a therapy dyad, a family, or a family in treatment would each be expected to exhibit its own particular developmental uniformities in its action system.

Though many uniformities deriving from social system properties of groups have been documented by sociologists, we were especially interested in the developmental properties of systems, like, for example, "phase movement" in Bales' (1953) problem-solving groups and "differentiation" in two-person psychotherapy groups (Lennard and Bernstein, 1960). As members of a group get to know each other and press toward the goals set for a system, a trend toward behavior specialization among group members characteristically seems to occur as a natural function of the group process. Concepts such as phase, differentiation, and equilibrium can readily be applied to describe these dynamic elements of system change.

The developmental and systems view allows the structure of the group process over time to be identified and provides a basis for generating hypotheses as to the direction that changes in group action will take. For example, the proposition that compensatory equilibrium mechanisms persist from one social contact to the next leads to the expectation that each member of a group will sooner or later participate in a group process. Similarly, from the systems theory perspective, it can be predicted that a systematic variation in the movement of the thematic focus of a group will occur such that the progression of discussion will move from the surface to more deeply emotional themes.

From the point of view of the psychological orientation, the determinants of group action processes are primarily a function of the personal and psychological attributes of individual members that compose a group. Individual personality differences certainly do play a role, at least initially, in determining an individual's behavior in a group. And such behavior on the part of an individual group member can, in some measure, affect the behavioral configuration of the entire group. The presence of a manic patient, a screaming mother, or a crying child forces those present in the same interactional field to attend to the themes and behaviors that such individuals introduce. In cases like these, interaction in a group will revolve around the single dominating member of the group.

Some individual attributes or characteristics may be more salient than others in determining what might be called their *interactional power* or potential. The more primitive an individual's needs are, or the more "drive-involved" they are, the more power they may exercise upon others in a group to attend to them either behaviorally or verbally. But an individual's ability to move the focus of a group process in his direction can also be a function of more mature personality attributes, such as dominance or perseverance.

Although the evolution and unfolding of group process is not normally affected by variations in the personalities of the members of a group, in unusual and limiting conditions, disturbances in the personality of a group member may have a considerable impact on group processes. For instance, the presence of a mute catatonic in a group or an extremely talkative and uncontrollable group member may ultimately force group norms so far beyond their limits that normal developmental and equilibrating processes cannot occur. But though knowledge of an individual's personality sometimes allows one to predict successfully how that individual might usually be expected to behave, such knowledge does not allow one to predict how *others* will react to him, nor to predict the extent to which his behavior will attract the attention and involvement of other group members. What a person says or does is important, but so also is *where* he says it and *when,* that is, the context in which the behavior occurs.

A third perspective then must be applied, one that reconciles transient group interactional configurations derived from members' psychological attributes with the more pervasive developmental and equilibrating phenomena that underlie group interaction processes such as those identified within the sociological frame of reference.

Proceeding from such an interactional perspective makes it

possible to formulate a series of research questions about individuals in interaction, the action process, and the social system or context in which action occurs. One set of questions might be the following: How is the rate and direction of action determined? How does social context, on the one hand, and psychological attributes of group members, on the other, influence the rate and direction of group members during specific system phases?

Another set of questions might revolve around configurations of action. For example, do different social contexts generate special interactional fields? How are interactional configurations in the same kind of system (for example, family) influenced by variations in the psychological characteristic of one or more of the members (for example, psychological disturbance in a child)? Further, how do social contexts differ from each other in terms of the scheduling and sequences of action over time, and do the *same contexts* composed of members having *different attributes* differ in such sequential parameters? And finally, can we identify those characteristics of interactional fields that are therapeutic or beneficial as against those that must be conceived of as damaging and pathogenic? The studies to be reported here wrestle with the conceptual and methodological issues involved in the consideration of these questions, and hopefully will throw some light on these questions.

From the perspective of the interactional approach to the study of human behavior, and especially its application to the study of mental illness, one further question seems relevant: To what extent does the behavior of a given patient (and his symptomatology) remain fixed and invariant, irrespective of the social or interactional setting in which he is participating?

Investigators of psychopathology often proceed as if they believed patients to be constrained to behave in a fixed way, regardless of the social context or the role relationship in which they are participating. Accordingly, some researchers are satisfied to construct profiles of a so-called schizophrenic patient's behavior patterns on the basis of assessments of his performances with only one role partner. Yet observers, psychiatrists, and behavioral scientists alike have noted that in the interaction patterns of patients there occurs a wide range of variability that seems to be contingent upon the context, type of role relationship, and system phase in which the patients are interacting.

SOCIAL SETTING AND BEHAVIOR

Part of the confusion arises from the different relative salience attributed to individual and to social determinants. Schemes of psychiatric classification often emphasize individual psychological attributes and exclude the part played by role and system determinants, rather than attempting to assess the relative contribution each plays in determining a patient's patterns of interpersonal behavior. Differences in psychiatric opinion about diagnoses in individual cases may therefore arise as much from differences in the interaction and context in which the diagnosis is made as from differences in the personality structure of the patient.

Patients behave differently with some people than with others and behave differently in some contexts than in others. Freud's (1911) discussion of the famous "Schreber Case" provides an intriguing illustration of this phenomenon. Schreber's extraordinary paranoid illness and delusional system (redemption of the world through his transformation into a woman) so intrigues Freud that he makes it the subject of a comprehensive exploration of the mechanisms of paranoia. Yet Schreber, according to his physician, engages in "normal" and "proper" interactions with others within an important everyday social context. Freud cites (without comment) the following remarks of Schreber's physician (Dr. Weber):

> Since for the last nine months Herr President Schreber has taken his meals daily at my family board, I have had the most ample opportunity of conversing with him upon every imaginable topic. . . . [I]n his lighter talk with the ladies of the party, he was both courteous and affable . . . *never once** during those innocent talks around the dining table, did he introduce subjects which should more properly have been raised at a medical consultation (p. 394).

This issue of variability in behavior as a function of context

* Italics added.

is presently receiving considerably more systematic examination and study than it ever has before. It is especially important that this examination be done, since assumptions about degrees of behavioral variability are unquestionably involved in decisions about diagnosis, therapy, and social policy concerning patients suffering from severe mental disorders. Researchers in psychiatric settings owe a debt to Stanton and Schwartz (1954) for their convincing documentation of the relevance of role and system factors to the manifestations of individual psychopathology and for demonstrating the feasibility of sociopsychiatric (clinical sociological) study of ongoing social processes.

How does one account for the observation that behavior (even in patients) can vary so much from setting to setting?

As we have seen, the sociological position views behavior as contingent upon context. From this viewpoint, individual variability in behavior from setting to setting is generated by social interaction. As individuals move from setting to setting they conform to the diverse, or even antithetical norms, of each different social context.

A number of sociologists (Goffman, 1961; Scheff, 1966) have been intrigued with the application of this sociological model to the problem of mental illness. In their view, the behaviors, symptoms, and performances of so-called mentally ill people can be viewed as forms of social deviance that follow upon, rather than precede, the diagnosis (labeling) of an individual as mentally ill. Advocates of this position believe that by refraining from attaching the label and role of patient to potential patients and that by providing a "healthy" social context in which the role of the "sick" person is absent, such an interactional context will be sufficient to restore the relevant behavior to the potentially "mentally ill" person.

It seems to us that this viewpoint likewise fails to take into account a considerable body of clinical observation and work, because it implicitly rejects the need for models of intrapsychic structure and because it employs an oversimplified interactional and contextual model. Psychopathology may be viewed as related to certain attributes of the interpersonal situation as well as to predisposing vulnerabilities and deficits "inside" the individual.

A more inclusive model would conceive of symptom-expressive behavior as a response of a person to a situation. The expression and intensity of psychopathological behavior may be triggered by the behavior, feelings, and demands of the coparticipant in an interaction or when communicational parameters transcend certain thresholds. For example, consider the following illustration. A young man, who has had a difficult adolescence, functions effectively away from home in a college setting. He is met by his mother upon his arrival home for a vacation. When his request to drive the car from the airport is denied by his mother, he has an uncontrollable hysterical outburst, which results in his mother's concerned telephone call to his therapist regarding her son's "apparent" psychological disturbance.

There is a relationship between the demands that role partners make upon each other and their ability to meet them. For example, if a slow, perhaps slightly retarded, student is placed in a competitive school situation with a demanding and impatient teacher, the emotional disturbance produced by characteristics of that setting and its role demands may exacerbate his intellectual impairment. In a now classic paper, Searles (1959) outlines a variety of interpersonal approaches that may result in "driving the other person crazy." He mentions the effect of persistence in forcing somebody to attend to aspects of a relationship or to feelings and thoughts that are unacceptable to them. For example, consider a man who constantly emphasizes sexuality with a sexually inhibited girl who has come to value other than the sexual aspects of their relationship. Here the demand to attend to feelings and sensations that have been excluded from awareness for "good" reasons may produce psychopathological phenomena (such as conversion symptoms and the like).

A number of factors must be taken into consideration if one is to account more fully for the behavioral variability that occurs in different contexts. We have assumed that there are differential "thresholds" for interacting within given communicational environments, specifically for the processing of given communications (hostile, deceptive, demeaning, and so on) and for adapting to given demands (for example, for unavailable or unacceptable performances), and for maintaining interaction in chaotic or unstable interactional environments. Some individuals are better able than others to adjust to diversity when contextual conditions require behavioral responses to fall within a range of acceptable forms of behavior. Such thresholds are not constant, and for some (whom we call psychiatrically ill) they are exceeded in some contexts. Some social settings are particularly able to generate excessively skewed communicational environments (see Section on Harmony and Discordance in Family Systems). Both the character of the communicational environment and the individual's "thresholds" for interaction within it are required to explain the emergence of psychopathology and the variability in the appearance of illness in different social settings.

INTERACTIONAL SEQUENCES AND BEHAVIOR

In the study of interaction among disturbed and delinquent youngsters in a residential setting, Rausch (1965) found that one of the best predictors of their interaction (for example, whether it would be friendly or hostile) was the nature of their preceding interaction. Knowing specifically what had previously transpired between members of a social group proved to be a better predictor of behavior, Rausch found, than knowing about either individual personality characteristics or the nature of the situation. Through the study of a specific role relationship, over a limited time span, using a quantitative approach, Rausch and his collaborators add concrete empirical evidence to our more general theoretical proposal that a broad, multidimensional, social psychological or interactional viewpoint is required for the complete elucidation of group processes.

However, this finding—that a particular characteristic of an interaction at Time 1 effects the characteristics of an interaction at Time 2—does not cast any light upon the nature of interactive relationships that are involved. Two models of interaction must be considered. One could be termed the "reactive" model (following Bales, (1953) in which interaction at a subsequent time (T_s) is seen as a reaction or response to the characteristics of a prior interaction process (at T_p). Such a model, which involves long interaction chains rather than immediate action-reaction sequences, is proposed in Bales' (1953) equilibrium model. In this view, for example, an excess of controlling communications would over the long run be balanced by an increase in negative reactions; and an excess of questions, by answers.

In this view, the allocation of action within social systems changes as the system develops or moves closer to the execution of the task for which it has been instituted. There is, however, a clear implication of an interdependence between phases or sequence units of the system. This relationship of subsequent distributions of actions to earlier states of the action process is accounted for in terms of concepts such as reaction and compensation.

A second model of the interaction process takes account of *cumulative* effects and suggests the term *stochastic process*. It may be illustrated by an example: A man who is trying to get out of a crowded parking lot may initially be observed as careful in his moves, making way for other cars and in good humor. He remains unaggressive in the face of contradictory directions and commands coming to him from other impatient drivers. After a series of episodes, however, he becomes less careful, less willing to let others pass and less willing to be told whether to move forward or back. Finally, he loses his temper (passes a stochastic threshold) and drives recklessly through the traffic, shouting at the other drivers to move here and there. An observer coming upon the scene at this time might infer that the driver was an unstable person, with little control over his impulses and reckless in his disregard for the rights and safety of himself and others.

This model, involving a cumulative effect, appears to be relevant to the understanding of many interaction systems. It seems to apply especially well to family interactions involving either husband and wife or parents and children. With regard to the latter, consider a parent's instruction to a child to clean his room, which is repeatedly disregarded. The longer the parent's command is ignored, the more likely the parent is to lose his temper and start to scold. An observer's judgment of a given parent's patience and stability would depend upon what phase of the interaction he witnessed—whether he was there from the start or happened on the scene at a late phase in the sequence of disregarded instructions. The cumulative effect model seems relevant to the understanding of social interaction processes in general.

At least four frames of reference need to be included in an analysis of behavioral variability in different contexts: (1) the type and structure of the social setting or contexts; (2) predisposing vulnerabilities and deficits, which could be conceived of as "inside" or pertaining to the individual; (3) the distribution and balances of communicative behaviors; and (4) the system sequence or phase in which the behavior is located.

TRAJECTORY OF INTERACTION

How can one conceptualize the shape and form of an inter-actional process as it moves through time, especially with respect to changes in its direction and rate? Interaction processes may revolve around different persons, behavior, and themes, and may exhibit the phenomena of acceleration and deceleration (as measured by varying rates of interaction).

The direction that interaction takes may be compared to trajectory—what we would like to describe as the trajectory of interaction. An interactional trajectory might be traced by following the course of changes that occur in the thematic focus of a group's attention. If interaction among people is limited to verbal inter-changes, then these thematic foci will revolve around ideas, topics, and persons. A focus of interaction might be somebody's behavior, for example, a child's misbehavior at the dinner table. Interaction in such a social context might "take off" from this theme and focus around modifying the child's behavior in order to permit interaction to continue in another direction, such as a decision to be made by the parents. The duration of such an interactional sequence would be a function of the variety of vectors acting in the social system at that time—the parent's expectations, the child's "resistance," the phase of the system.

Parsons (1956) suggests that the concept of motivational power is the social science equivalent of the concept of mass in classical mechanics. Following this suggestion, one should be able to predict how long an individual will engage in a specific course of behavior or will pursue a given theme if one knew how strongly motivated that individual is to do so. Conversely, one can often infer the intensity of motivation by noticing how persevering an individual is in pursuing a theme and how long it will take him to "run out of steam." Other group members may either permit or interfere with the ongoing focus, reflecting, in turn, the intensity of their motivations in pursuing another theme or in redirecting the focus to another person's behavior (often their own).

One may view the direction of action in a social field as somewhat analogous to the trajectory of an object that has been propelled, thrown, or ejected. The direction and velocity of such an object is determined by the force with which the object is released, the angle, and the forces that oppose its movement. For example, if we consider predicting the course of a baseball, we would need to know its weight, the force with which it is propelled, its initial angle and the air currents operating in the ball field, and, of course, the positions of the ball players in the path of the ball. Following the changes in the thematic focus of a group's attention is somewhat like following a baseball as it travels among the players during a ball game.

By following the course of action in social groups one is enabled to observe "who carries the ball," for how long, and how frequently and to whom "the ball is thrown." This observing permits an assessment of the relative commitment of the participants to various thematic and behavioral foci as well as to persons. Furthermore, it provides information on the relative power or skill of individual group members in deflecting and controlling action processes set into motion by others.

INTERACTIONAL POTENTIAL

A given kind of behavior or a given kind of problem will attract more attention and generate more involvement on the part of group members in some contexts than in others. The ability of an

instance of behavior or a problem to attract attention or involvement, that is to say, to generate interaction, we shall refer to as its
interactional potential.

The interactional potential of a group member's behavioral
contribution resides in its ability to generate involvement of other
group members. Such involvement may be made manifest by an
increase in the number of group members who attend to the person
contributing the behavior or to the content of that behavior. This
involvement may take the form of a snowballing of interest or of
perseverance in pursuit of the theme introduced. Interactional potential does not reside in an action or in an actor, but in the interaction between them and the other respondents as well as the situation.

The interactional potential of a given behavior or a given
person to act as a thematic rallying point for a group is not constant
throughout the life of a group. Rather, interactional potential varies
with the developmental or evolutionary stage of the group. For example, the ability of a therapy group to exhibit a high rate of group
participation in interaction focused upon one member's expression
of rage against authority can occur only after the group has progressed to a phase in its development in which communication about
feeling has replaced intellectual discussions, and at a time when the
members of the group have already progressively become more in-
tensely involved in participation.

INTERACTION AS FUNCTION OF MOTIVATION

Some individuals appear to be motivated to interact with
more individuals than others, some for longer periods of time, and
some at higher interaction rates than others. Moreover, as we shall
see, even the same individual appears to vary his rate of interaction
from time to time. Both psychological and sociological determinants
may account for these individual variations.

Insofar as an individual has the option to initiate interaction,
to allow others to interact with him, or to refrain from contact with
others, he may control his own degree of interaction. However, in
many social contexts, the rate, extent, and kinds of interaction are

controlled by the context, which may allow for only a minimum of variation. Sometimes an individual seeks out or chooses settings because of their interactional requirements, since they might experience discomfort in settings in which the interactional demands exceed or fall below their preferred rate. In many settings interactions are prescribed (for example, professors are required to have some contact with students outside of the classroom), though considerable option may still be exercised as to with whom and for how long such interaction has to be engaged in (professors interact more with some students than with others).

Some students of human behavior attribute variations among interaction rates to individual differences in operant activity levels. Individuals are viewed as possessing different energy levels and their individual rates of interaction are thought to derive from these. The work of Chapple *et al.* (1960) represents an attempt to document such differences in activity output.

Lowered activity levels are sometimes ascribed to the effect of mental illness such as depression and schizophrenia. A depressed patient shows a reduced rate of physical movement and participation in social situations with others. Yet careful observation shows that even for a depressed patient decrease in activity is not distributed equally among all situations or with all role partners, but rather that he avoids some settings and interactions more than others.

While it is self-evident that individuals differ in the amount of interaction they engage in, the problem is to account for *intra*-individual variations in interaction rates, why individuals interact more with some role partners than with others. We may cast some light on this question by observing some of the general functions served by interaction. If, for example, one function of interaction is the acquisition of information, then it follows that whoever is likely to have the sought-for information will become an object of increased interaction. This possibility suggests an even more general proposition about the motivational function of interaction: that persons seek interaction in order to be responded to, to elicit a response. A sought-for response may be unspecific, that is, a request for any kind of return communication (for example, the prisoner in the cell adjoining Rubashoff's in Koestler's (1961) *Darkness at Noon*).

But when the characteristics of the sought-for response are defined in advance, there is likely to be a tendency to increase interaction with those who are most likely to provide that response.

One general proposition that can be offered about responses that lead to the recurrence of interaction is that such responses tend to authenticate or affirm something about the persons engaged in the interaction—an aspect either of the self-concept or of the self presented in the interaction. ("Look Ma, I'm dancing!") These responses may involve significant aspects of the role conceptions held by the particular status occupants. For example, a professor who sees himself, and wishes to be seen, as a "scholar" or "discoverer of new knowledge," would, in terms of this formulation, tend to interact with those students whose communications affirm this specialized conception of his role. Students who consult him about personal problems or a choice of courses may find him unavailable, while those faced by a research problem or who are intrigued by a theoretical question, may find him ready for lengthy and recurrent interaction.

This view of interaction is advanced by the playwright, Genet, who suggests that an appropriate response fulfills a function more basic than that of sustaining interaction. It also serves to maintain the identity of the participants in their respective roles. Without reinforcement from others, an individual has difficulty in regarding himself as occupying a particular role. For example, consider this passage from Genet's (1960) *The Balcony*.

> JUDGE: . . . My being a judge is an emanation of your being a thief. You need only refuse—but you'd better not!—need only refuse to be who you are—what you are therefore, who you are—for me to cease to be . . . to vanish, evaporate. Lord, I beseech you. Don't leave me in this position failing to be a judge (pp. 14–15).

Chapter 3

Methodological Problems

$\mathcal{J}\mathcal{U}\mathcal{J}\mathcal{U}\mathcal{J}\mathcal{U}\mathcal{J}\mathcal{U}\mathcal{J}\mathcal{U}\mathcal{J}\mathcal{U}\mathcal{J}\mathcal{U}\mathcal{J}\mathcal{U}\mathcal{J}\mathcal{U}\mathcal{J}\mathcal{U}\mathcal{J}\mathcal{U}\mathcal{J}\mathcal{U}\mathcal{J}$

When attention is shifted from the behavior of individuals to the recurrent behavior inter-changes *between* individuals, the lack of applicability of prevailing theoretical perspectives, concepts, and methods of study to description and to intervention, becomes readily apparent. Inadequacies in existing theories and methods, especially those derived primarily from individual and depth psychology, require the invention of new approaches and new descriptive terms to meet the specifications of this new theoretical reorientation. The objective of such conceptual and methodological innovations is to bring into view and to focus upon the wider arrays of interpersonal behavior that take place in social systems.

PROBLEMS OF DESCRIPTION

Anyone who has ever undertaken to describe even the most casual of interpersonal encounters confronts almost insurmountable difficulties of summary, selection, and omission. If the complexity of human phenomena and the richness of our own perception and inner commentary appear too overwhelming to be completely described, even in a fleeting contact between two strangers, then how much more formidable the task becomes when it involves describing interaction in a relationship with an extended history, in which each utterance or act is imbued with the surplus meanings inhering from many previous behavior exchanges. Only after we have set ourselves a specific task or have had one assigned to us can we accomplish a reasonably coherent account of what is transpiring even within a limited time period.

The almost infinite variety of ways of describing complex human phenomena forces upon one the recognition that no single description will suffice; nor will it reveal the "ultimate" structure of these phenomena. But rather, as in Kaplan's (1964) view, we must assume a structure to the world that is independent of our conceptualization of it, and then construct theories that have a relationship to this structure—enough of a relationship so that we can use them like a map to get from place to place. A theory is to be regarded as a tool or an instrument. Thus, theories and concepts about interpersonal behavior in social systems should be treated as orienting devices toward interactional phenomena. As Merton (1957) says about general sociological theory, "Such orientations involve broad postulates which indicate *types* of variables which are somehow to be taken into account rather than specifying determinate relationships between particular variables (p. 88)."

LEVELS OF DESCRIPTION

When one applies the frameworks, concepts, and methods that have been developed to study human interaction, one must examine the ways in which those concepts relate to the actual phenomena they purport to describe. Concepts and frameworks can be ordered in terms of the implicit number of inferences they require. The number of inferences required to bridge the distance between a concept and the actual interactional phenomenon it is designed to describe may be large or small. Some concepts refer to processes that can be assessed and studied without requiring much inference; for example, the concept of "activeness" (Chapple *et al.*, 1960). Others may require considerably more tolerance of inference by an investigator; for example, a concept such as the "double-bind" (Bateson *et al.*, 1956). Conceptualizations of interaction also vary with regard to the size, duration, and complexity of the behavioral segments they delimit. As the segment of behavior embraced within a concept increases in size and complexity, the amount of inference involved in applying the concept may also increase.

Concepts may be hierarchically related to each other, referring to cumulatively more complex aspects of behavior, which represent more and more abstract or complex formulations about the same phenomenon. A simple illustration is the relationship among the concepts of act, role behavior, and system of role relationships. For example, in our studies we focus on *particular communicative acts* such as information-giving, agreement, disagreement, and questions. But we also employ descriptions of behavior in terms of *role*. The concept of role refers to a *configuration of acts* that accompany status occupancy (for example, husband or therapist). To move up to still more complex levels of description, such as *role systems,* requires the fitting together of patterns of role behaviors. Particular acts, therefore, are included within the relatively more complex concept of role behavior, which is subsumed under the still more complex concepts of system and social processes. In practice, theorists or researchers working within different levels of conceptualization may utilize several levels of description at the same time.

CONCEPTS AND CONCEPT INDICATORS

Discussions in social science research literature also revolve around the relationship of a "concept" to its "indicators." Lazarsfeld and Barton (1951) and others remind us that it is one thing to formulate a set of theoretical concepts for the description of a phenomenon, but quite another thing to select and design, for such concepts, "indicators" that can be measured (for example, actions, verbalizations, performances). Obviously, an indicator should be less complex than the concept it purports to operationalize, and should require less inference for the purpose of classification and measurement. Take, for example, the concept of the communication barrier. To study communication barriers, one must define a set of concept indicators. If "not to answer somebody" and "not to address somebody" are regarded as indicators of a communication barrier, then it becomes a relatively simple matter to count such indicators.

The number of concept indicators needed to describe a process or a phenomenon varies. Two or three indicators (lack of verbal interaction, bodily withdrawal, and the like) might well be considered sufficient to represent the presence or absence of communication barriers in a family; but so few indicators may not be sufficient to identify and measure the characteristics of homeostatic processes.

In this book we have selected certain concepts that have been widely regarded by clinicians and by social scientists as significant for understanding family and therapy interactions, and have attempted to define indicators for such concepts. These indicators were used to enable us to gather data relevant to significant theoretical and conceptual frameworks that have been used to account for interaction and social behavior of both so-called normal individuals and those diagnosed as mentally ill.

If in our study of interaction processes we tend to place greater emphasis upon the formal and process characteristics of interactions than upon their contents, it is because these characteristics are not usually accorded the attention they deserve, but also because we suspect that Hare (1961) may be right when he argues that the *form* of interaction frequently turns out to be a major factor, even in research devoted to content.

ASSESSMENT OF RESEARCH METHODS

Students of the family, of therapy, and of other social contexts employ a variety of research methods. Among the methods

most frequently used are clinical description, interview and questionnaire methods, self-report, experimentation, and systematic analysis
of ongoing interaction processes through observation or categorization of records of such processes. In the research to be reported in
this book, we have worked with a combination of these methods,
but we were especially interested in developing quantitative methods
for the analysis of ongoing behavior processes; therefore, before
moving on to a discussion of our own preferences and the specific
methodology we selected, we will briefly review some of the advantages and disadvantages of the various methods of behavior
study mentioned above.

CLINICAL IMPRESSION AND DESCRIPTION

Clinical description represents the main vehicle of communication among members of a clinical team, between a therapist
(whether a psychiatrist, a psychologist, or a social worker) and his
supervisor, and between teachers of clinical practice and their students. However, the language and vocabulary of clinical description varies with different theoretical viewpoints.

The language used by clinicians certainly constitutes a very
rich resource for communication among professionals about behavioral phenomena because it allows them the latitude to use an
array of expressions, metaphors, and allusions. Clinical descriptions
of interpersonal behavior can be couched, for emphasis, in both
scientific and folk idiom. When a description is offered by one who
is himself a participant in an interaction, the reporter has the added
advantage of access to his own reactions and the feelings generated
in him by "being in the situation," and he can sometimes give voice
to his perception of subtle and fleeting interactional phenomena
that might otherwise escape notice.

These very virtues of clinical observation, description, and
reporting, however, also represent one of their major drawbacks as a
research instrument. For the very freedom of choice open to those
offering clinical descriptions of interactional phenomena militates
against different observers being able to agree on how (in what
terms and within which conceptual framework) the phenomena
under observation are to be talked about. Expressions of subtle

personal reactions are often too obscure to be precisely understood by someone outside of the setting being observed. But perhaps more importantly, human interaction process being so fleeting, so ephemeral, and so infinitely complex, even the most experienced and attentive observer will be unable to apprehend and report (without adequate instrumentation) most of the interactional phenomena likely to be encountered in any given segment of interpersonal behavior. The more involved the participant-observer becomes in the human interaction he is studying, the narrower will be the range of phenomena he can attend to at any one time.

INTERVIEW AND QUESTIONNAIRE METHODS

Interview and questionnaire methods are frequently employed in studies of social systems when these studies are undertaken by and from the perspective of behavioral science. Most studies of socialization and child-rearing patterns in American families rely upon lengthy interviews and questionnaire schedules administered to family members. Studies of individual personality attributes and behavior of individuals in various social settings also rely heavily on these means. This approach permits data collection from a large number of families. The family members can be utilized as informants and can be asked to report upon events that have transpired within the family over the course of months or years. The interview schedule in such studies can cover a gamut of behaviors, relationships, and reactions. The type of data yielded by such survey approaches is readily translatable into quantitative terms and permits the application of most sophisticated statistical and machine processing procedures.

One major problem we faced in applying the survey approach to achieve the purposes of the investigations pursued in this volume was the poor fit between the action-process phenomena we wished to study and the conceptual and linguistic framework in which these action processes would have to be reported were a questionnaire-survey approach to be employed. For example, reporting a form of maternal behavior as "intrusive," while within the common linguistic discourse of informant and investigator, would not really provide any data on the actual allocations and sequences of behaviors that occurred within the family, which were subsumed under such a response.

This comment should not be mistaken for the more traditional objection to the use of survey approaches—for example, Mills' (1963) observation that the disparity between talk and action constitutes the central methodological problem of the social sciences. This criticism refers to the likelihood that subjects, interviewees, informants, and the like will be unable or unwilling to report accurately, and cannot help presenting a distorted picture of interactional processes in which they have participated.

It is the *inability* of informants to report on what we wish to study that is the most serious drawback of the interview approach for our purposes. For it is just as difficult for a person engaged in interaction to be simultaneously aware of the multiple aspects of interaction process as to monitor nuances of grammar and syntax of speech while engaged in a heated political discussion. The temporal vicissitudes of interaction process are especially resistant to awareness. "Both changes in behavioral process that occur much more quickly than the average tempo of interaction, and those that occur more slowly, tend to elude conscious awareness and control (Bales, 1960, p. ix)."

Even the interview or a meeting in which a questionnaire is administered is itself a special social context with its own normative and demand structures and its own interactional system requirements. Verbal reporting represents a behavioral contribution by one of the members of an interview context. The behavioral contributions of members of any context are influenced by the system and process variables as well as by the expectations that are operative in that context. Hence, the behavioral contributions of the members participating in an interview interaction system may be as much a function of the interactional requirements and interactional structure of the interview context as of the other social context (family or whatever) to which the interview is addressed. For example, a typical interview context is differentiated from other social contexts by virtue of the fact that information must be divulged to a "stranger." One would then expect to find phases in the over-time characteristics of an interview system in which the amount and kind of self-disclosures made by interviewees changed over time. These phases would be parallel to the changes in the patterning of interaction that occur within the life of all social systems. One would anticipate that the interpersonal relationship, the interaction process, and the type of information revealed would be very different in later interviews conducted by the same interviewer and informant than in the initial encounter. It should also be expected that the context in which an interview is embedded (for example, research or diagnosis) would influence its structure and content.

These considerations need not necessarily discourage attempts to study family, therapy, and social contexts by means of interviews and questionnaires. But they do require that the assumptions underlying this mode of data collection be examined. One way of examining this mode would be through the design of studies in which the same interactional phenomena would be tracked through observation, interviews, and systematic analysis of tape or filmed records of the interactions. Comparing these data might throw light upon which of the different methods yield the least and the most comparable information about which of the dimensions and processes. Likewise, efforts invested in the development of interaction inventories oriented to the study of family groups or ward behavior and other therapeutic contexts should not be dismissed as unrewarding. Final judgment as to which methods or which combination of methods will be the most fruitful in the study of the patterning of ongoing social interaction should be withheld until considerably more research has been completed.

EXPERIMENTAL APPROACH

Specific parameters of human interaction and social relationship systems can be studied under controlled conditions through the setting up of experimental groups. Such studies were first carried on with ad hoc and experimentally constituted social groups but have now been introduced into the study of family dynamics in both "normal" and "abnormal" families. Some investigators recommend the adoption of this methodology for the exploration of parameters considered significant in the study of psychotherapy contexts.

The interpretation of findings obtained by the experimental

method, it has been suggested, does not require so much inference and is subject to less distortion than data acquired by other methods such as clinical description, interviewing, or categorization of stored interaction process data; but, without wishing to disparage in any way the development of family experiments, we must suggest that this approach creates its own problems and raises new questions that it is unable to answer.

One such question relates to the comparability of the "languages" used in experiments to the medium used in "natural" social interaction. How, for example, is family interaction in an experimental setting constrained by the experimental "language" (such as playing a game, pushing buttons, or passing notes without speaking) used in such settings? Experimentation provides a new medium of interaction and, to paraphrase McLuhan (1966), the medium not only contains messages but also constrains messages. A cursory examination of some of the messages passed among family members in a "family experiment" makes it appear that certain kinds of content (for example, messages dealing with affect) are not likely to be contained in such notes. Moreover, the use of "pushing a button" as an indicator of "dominance" in a family seems to us to require no less inference than that one must use when he locates a verbal exchange in a category such as "disagreement."

Nonetheless, the experimental approach to the study of "natural" interaction should be encouraged. Again, we consider it important to compare the different kinds of information yielded about a given social system when different methods are employed, such as systematic observation, self-report, or experiment.

QUANTITATIVE ANALYSIS

In our judgment, the patterns in human interaction processes are not fully accessible to clinical description, no matter how informed or skilled the clinician may be; nor can complete and accurate information about such processes be elicited by interviews and questionnaires. The main thrust of our effort consequently turned to the development of methods of quantitative analysis of stored interaction process data—that is, written, taped, and filmed records of interaction. We hold with Bales (1960) that such ". . . a

quantitative approach may help to bring within cognitive grasp
changes and relationships that otherwise escape attention . . . (p.
ix)."

Such a quantitative approach involves the detailed assessment and measurement (through sets of interrelated categories) of
social interaction processes. In this approach each communicative
act, as well as shorter and longer sequences of interaction, is evalu-
ated and coded along a number of dimensions derived from conceptual frameworks considered to be significant in the study of
interaction. The numerical data obtained in this fashion can subsequently be summarized and manipulated in a variety of ways designed to elucidate the structure and evolution of interactional phenomena.

The advantages of this approach may be illustrated by anal-
ogy to the medical specialty of epidemiology. The epidemiologist,
often not a practicing physician, does not aspire to the level of understanding brought to the study of a sick individual by a clinical
specialist. But, as Morris (1957) writes, ". . . the epidemiologist
can sometimes ask questions which the clinician also asks, and get
different (maybe better, maybe worse) information in reply." He
goes on to say that "Often, the epidemiologist may ask questions
that cannot be asked in clinical medicine at all (p. 3)" because
understanding is facilitated by the collection and analysis of data
from a large number of cases. The effect of thalidomide on embryo
deformity serves as an illustration. It would not have been reasonable to expect even the most brilliant diagnostician when encounter-
ing one or two deformed babies to specify etiology and to implicate
a particular process or chemical consumed by the mother as a
cause of infant deformity. However, information on the drug
consumption patterns of *many* mothers could—and did—provide
significant leads. The position we suggest is similar to the one advanced by the epidemiologist. We contend that the kind of methodology employed here may yield a level of insight different from and,
hopefully, complementary to that provided by clinical study.

The advantages of quantitative analysis as employed in the
studies reported in this book appear to us to be many. By working
with stored interaction process data, we are able to subject the same

interactional data to repeated examination. Weeks or months can be spent in scrutinizing and measuring small segments of interaction process. While even the most skilled observer is limited in the scope of his observation (he can, for example, work with only one category system at a time), the student of stored process data can re-analyze his data on the basis of multiple categorizations. He can assume different perspectives toward the same phenomena to learn which perspective makes the most sense.

Clinicians, observers, and participants find it difficult to capture behavioral processes that occur more quickly or more slowly than the average tempo of social interaction. The quantitative analyst may literally speed up or slow down the process or change the size of the unit under study. He can opt for an examination of small, minute segments of interaction process or study larger and more lasting sequences of interaction. Furthermore, after arriving at an evaluation or assessment, he can apply previously developed sets of rules, and compare his application of such rules with those of his colleagues or critics.

USE OF CATEGORY SYSTEMS

Quantitative analysis of interaction process involves the development of observational or content analytic category systems. Some general remarks are thus in order about the purposes that are served in the study of human behavior—specifically, by the development of category systems and by the act of classifying per se. Category systems permit students of human behavior to summarize diverse observations and to separate out common aspects in complex behavioral data. Thus, actual coding or categorization makes analysis of the "stream of behavior" a more manageable objective.

The reduction of complex "living" data by common sets of categories permits comparisons between systems and between social contexts. Indeed, Bales (1950), who is the creator of perhaps the most widely used set of categories for analysis of social interaction, explains that he was motivated to undertake this task so as to provide students of small groups with measures somewhat analogous to those available to students of large social structures in the form of rates and indices (for example, suicide, crime, birth, death, and divorce rates). In this way, overall comparisons could be made not only between different kinds of systems, but also between specific dimensions. In comparing distributions of behavior in different kinds of systems, similarities as well as differences emerge.

Category systems permit an investigator to test hypotheses regarding the presence or absence of specific interactional processes and sequences. As a variety of different behavioral data are worked through and scrutinized, new hypotheses may be generated. The act of developing a category system proceeds by stages, involving various conceptual tasks at each stage. The solving of conceptual problems progressively increases one's understanding of the relation between the raw data of human interaction and the theoretical frameworks that have been constructed to account for these data. Categories are often derived from prevailing theories and perspectives. The first step, then, is often to achieve an understanding of the diverse theories that have been advanced by clinicians and investigators, so that categories relevant to such theories can be appropriately constructed.

Once concepts have been translated into categories, the behavioral data must be closely examined, and numberless decisions must be made as to which verbal acts and which behaviors are subsumed within a particular category. Very often one learns from this experience that categories are overlapping or are not really clear. Not only do the categories then have to be revised, but the investigator has to set down sets of rules that govern each act of classification, often having to provide illustrations of which behaviors fall into one or the other of the categories. Such efforts at description are extremely useful in helping a researcher learn what it is that he or a clinician is really talking about.

Like other learning experiences, the steps of defining categories and the procedure of classifying are painful, and not as immediately satisfying as the noble art of theorizing. This difficulty may well be one of the reasons why so few people have invested their effort in such activities. A search through the clinical and research literature on the family and other social systems will locate few comprehensive category systems, especially ones which are completely described and replete with definitions and indicators that make the system useful to other students.

Let us turn to some other methodological problems and decisions an investigator faces when he undertakes to develop a category system. First, shall he devise a system of categories that is limited to the system he is studying (for example, the family), or one that would also be applicable to a large number of social interaction systems? Our bias is toward the latter alternative. An all-purpose category system directed to the study of interaction contexts and relationship systems as such provides us with the possibility of seeing the similarities and differences in system functioning and variables that would not be available to an investigator who used research instruments specifically designed for the study of only *one* particular system. The category systems reported here, like those devised for family study by Wynne and Singer (1965), and Goldfarb and Meyers (1961), lend themselves (without much modification) to the study of diverse communication systems.

A further question that should be resolved is the comprehensiveness of the category system. Should it be inclusive enough to permit the assessment of multiple hypotheses? Or should it be restricted to the operationalizing and investigation of one set of concepts only? Since data collection in interaction research is a very time-consuming business, an epidemiological or survey research model is far more practical than the one-variable model favored by psychological investigators.

In long-term epidemiological studies, especially in the area of chronic illness, where there are many competing hypotheses and so little hard knowledge, information is obtained on a variety of relevant variables in the same study. The collection of a variety of data does not necessarily commit a researcher to analyze all of the data collected, but it permits separate analyses for each set of variables, and does not foreclose on the possibility of combining several approaches to the data in a subsequent analysis.

This strategy applies to the use of a multiple coding system in interaction analysis as well. For example, in the family studies we have undertaken, each verbalization contributed by a family member was classified along ten dimensions. We were subsequently in a position to carry through an analysis of the formal or process features of interaction separately from an analysis of content dimensions. In addition, we could combine elements of both analyses.

A number of general objections that have been raised with regard to the use of category systems might be briefly discussed. One is that the phenomenon of communication involves multiple channels, and category systems are limited to only one channel, usually the verbal one. A second and more serious objection is that the parameters selected for study and that are amenable to measurement are not really the significant ones.

Many clinicians are pessimistic about the utility and feasibility of undertaking a quantitative assessment of the "significant" parameters of interpersonal behavior. They do not feel that such parameters are accessible to measurement by any of the currently available methodologies or models. The phenomena of interpersonal behavior seem too complex and too subtle to be captured by atomistic techniques that do not, in their view, do justice to the whole picture of an ongoing human interaction. We do not share this pessimistic outlook (though we do share its skepticism) about the fruitfulness of approaching the data of human interaction systems through objective and quantitative techniques. At this stage of knowledge about family and therapy interaction systems there does not seem to be a consensus as to what the "significant" variables are. What seems to be called for first is a consensus on what methods could be employed to *discover* what these significant parameters and variables are.

A third criticism, which is certainly not unjustified, is that the reliability of category systems is often not adequate; that categories are often insufficiently well-defined and that the amount of inference involved in applying them is not substantially less than that of pure clinical judgments.

However, the degree to which these observations are valid often is a function of the purpose to which a category system is put. For example, there is a considerable body of interest in the study of family interaction that centers not on the "disturbed" family but on intrafamilial behavior in relation to socioeconomic ethnic or cultural differences. Whenever the objective is to study *gross* differences between systems, an inability to assess more subtle nuances of interaction may well be less significant. Only through continued attention to improving and refining sets of categories and systems of classification can this method achieve the degree of reliability required in the field of interaction research.

UNITIZATION OF INTERACTION PROCESS

Describing the flow of ongoing human interaction in a social system requires analysis of the behavior exchanged in that system in terms of segments and units. Without exception, psychiatric and sociological descriptions of behavior require the clinician or investigator employing them to make decisions regarding interactional units. Such decisions are likely to be made without the clinician's being aware of them; but they should, when possible, be made explicit, rather than remain implicit in the descriptive language. Frequently it is only after research using clinical concepts is undertaken that the problem of making the unit explicit becomes critical. For unless we can recognize and identify the boundaries of the phenomena referred to in the vocabularies of clinicians and behavioral scientists, we shall not be able to direct our attention to the same (in time and space) phenomena, and students of interaction will not be able to agree upon what they are describing. Unitization is, therefore, a problem that cannot be overlooked.

There has been considerable controversy on how the flow of interaction should be segmented, and discussion on both the advantages and the disadvantages of particular decisions regarding units. The problem has unfortunately become polarized around the issue of "natural" versus "artificial" units. Barker (1963), who is perhaps the most eloquent spokesman for the "natural" unit, argues that "natural" behavior units represent "self generated parts of the stream of behavior." He maintains that the boundaries of behavior units occur independently of the operations of the investigator and are easily recognizable by the participants in the social interaction process. Barker's data, however, do not fully support his notion that it is easy to recognize where one "natural" behavioral unit ends and where the next "natural" behavioral unit begins. Moreover, most large behavioral sequences are "natural" as a result of socialization processes and because of the pressure toward consensus that operates in social contexts. Barker's studies, in general, also tend to be global, and to be oriented more to physical than to verbal behavior. It is simpler to define the "natural" boundaries of behavior of the participants in a ball game (moving up to bat, pitching, stealing a base) than it is to define the "natural" boundaries of the units of interactional behavior among family members during a family argument.

The system of unitization of interaction process into social acts, proposed by Bales (1950) from Mead's (1934) perspective on social process, seems entirely consonant with an emphasis on "natural" units. An act, for Bales, is the smallest segment of interaction process an observer can categorize, that is, assign a meaning to, from the point of view of the person to whom the act is directed. With respect to verbal interaction, an act, therefore, would in the main overlap with a verbal proposition. It is reasonable to infer that to convey an item of information that can be interpreted requires a proposition containing both subject and predicate.

Perhaps one should discuss decisions on unitization* as they are made in clinical studies as distinct from those required in research involving some sort of systematic measurement. When a clinician discusses interpersonal behavior, his focus may shift from a single act, verbal or kinesic, to an incident, an episode, or a repetitive chain of actions and reactions. Within a clinical framework he is able to switch from one implicit unit to another without having to say so, or without having the task of spelling out either the temporal duration of the interactional phenomena he refers to or the particular configuration of verbal, paralinguistic, or kinesic communications he includes in his description. This observation is equally valid for the theoretical constructions of behavioral scientists who describe social behavior without delineating the boundaries of the behavioral events they are describing. On the other hand, the student of interactional behavior, committed to a more systematic

---

* For further discussion of "units" used in research on social interaction, see Miller (1963) and Scheflen (1965).

approach (though not necessarily quantitative), is forced, by the methods he has selected, to indicate his decisions about unitization, and is held accountable for those decisions.

A redefinition of units sometimes leads to the emergence of insights of considerable theoretical and practical consequence. For example, Stanton's and Schwartz's (1954) enlargement of the observation of patient disturbance in a mental hospital ward to encompass staff interaction relative to the patient, and especially staff disagreements regarding the patient, yielded significant insights on the interdependence of staff disagreement and patient disturbances.

In the studies reported in this book we worked with a variety of units, both "natural" and "arbitrary." However, we propose that a distinction between a "primary" and "derived" unit is more appropriate.

The smallest unit we employed in segmenting interaction process for the purposes of categorization and quantification is the *proposition,* defined as a verbalization containing a subject and predicate, whether expressed or implied. The next larger unit, a *statement,* refers to an uninterrupted sequence of propositions. Flow of interaction can also be seen as a series of *exchanges.* Each exchange or interaction consists of two successive statements. In studies of dyadic groups—such as therapist-patient—an exchange is a therapist statement followed by a patient statement, or vice versa. In studies of family interaction process an exchange encompasses a statement of one family member followed by a statement of another family member.

In the examination of interaction process in systems containing more than two members we had to develop triple and quadruple units of exchange. A triple-exchange unit is a reciprocal exchange between two system members (for example, mother to father followed by father to mother) followed by a statement by the third system member directed to either system member involved in the previous exchanges (son to either mother or father). A quadruple-exchange sequence requires an additional subsequent statement by one of the system members (father to son, mother to son, or father to mother).

The extension of the interactional unit to include triple and quadruple sequences is not so arbitrary as it appears, since the triple sequence can easily be recognized by the participants as a "conversational interruption," and the quadruple sequence may involve either a successful or unsuccessful interruption.

This extension of the boundaries of interactional units is perhaps analogous to those described by Murray (1951) under the heading of "interpersonal proceeding." Other investigators will, no doubt, extend the boundaries of interaction sequences even further as their conceptual frameworks or the requirements of ongoing research may demand.

DERIVED UNITS

Unitization and categorization are interrelated activities. Behavior can be categorized only when it is clear what is to be categorized, what the units are. Categorization permits the translation of the raw data into quantitative form, so that a numerical score or value can be assigned to a unit in terms of a category. In this way, data can be tabulated for purposes of analysis. Statistical analysis, however, allows the summarization or combination of such numerical scores or measures. Derived units represent such summaries of interaction process data. For example, when psychotherapy interaction data are summarized for subperiods within a session or for the session as a whole, a new unit is formed. Comparisons can then be made between sessions, and between the beginning and the conclusion of a session. Although such units are in some sense "natural," they are obtained through manipulation of derived scores and measurements, and therefore may be viewed as derived units.

The problem of unitization might very well be a problem of not seeing the forest for the trees. Data processing and greater perspective lend manageability and structure to the raw data of human interaction. Larger units of structure—pattern or configuration—may emerge only after smaller units are identified and ordered, much as a statistical correlation or a mean identifies among the data a relationship that might otherwise go unnoticed.

SAMPLING OF INTERACTION PROCESS

What slice of the life of a social system need one study in order to make valid inferences about its interactional structure and about the characteristic sequences of interaction processes prevailing in the system under study? Some investigators suggest that weeks or months of observation of a social system such as family or therapy is required before such inferences can plausibly be made. Others, like students of paralinguistic and kinesic interaction such as Birdwhistle (1960), maintain that characteristic patterns of interaction are revealed within a few minutes or less (see, for example, Pittenger, 1960).

With reference to family interaction, it appears to us that the issue cannot be settled in general, but only in relation to specific parameters of family structure and communication process. If, for example, an observer wishes to determine which family members are not speaking to each other, then an observation of even a brief interaction sequence that provides family members an opportunity to speak with each other may be an adequate sample. When the issue concerns the distribution or prevalence of kinds of behavior that are almost always required in any situation involving all family members (such as speaking with each other), it poses a different sampling problem than when the study concerns occasional and periodic behaviors. For example, if one were interested in family behavior directed toward socializing a child to his sex role, the problem of obtaining a valid sample of such behaviors would be more difficult. To decide on a sample, one would have to know how socializing acts are distributed over time and within settings. If such acts, for example, are likely to occur no less than once an average week and only within the home, then a sample observation of family process of less than one week's duration or outside of the home might not be sufficient. Unfortunately, systematic information that could be used as a guide for such determinations is not available and not likely to be for some time. The investigator is thus forced to use his judgment regarding the probable distribution of given behaviors and the representativeness of the picture of family process variables his sampling decision has yielded. Repeated observations of the same families that yield comparable results help increase his confidence in the soundness of his judgment.

STABILITY AND VARIABILITY

In order to sample interpersonal behavior in family or therapy settings and to establish the "reliability" of any one sample or group of samples, information is needed on the *stability* of such interactions for given periods of time, contexts, and role relationships. More specifically, one needs to know about the "stability" of the interactional parameters being assessed. For example, while distribution of overall activity among group members may turn out to be quite stable, the distribution of who *initiates* the activity in a group may vary considerably.

Whatever systematic information is presently available on stability and change in interaction patterns is based on "experimentally constituted" social systems and usually involves only the beginning phases of the relationship between group members. Two important exceptions are the work of Barker (1963) and his associates and some interesting but unpublished work by Wiggins (1955), which deal with the reliability intervals of different duration in the study of interview interaction. Our own research on psychotherapy interaction of neurotic office patients (Lennard and Bernstein, 1960) and a pilot study on psychotherapy with hospitalized schizophrenic patients do suggest stability in many parameters of interaction in therapy systems.

Theoretical statements and clinical observations on interaction process in general, and on interaction in specific social systems in particular, unfortunately leave the problem unsolved, since two divergent positions (postulating stability as well as instability) have been advanced. This issue is especially critical in the study of the "disturbed" family. The question to be answered is, generally, how stable are family interaction patterns over longer periods of time, especially over a span of years; and specifically which patterns are more stable than others and may therefore be assumed to have characterized interaction in a family *before* the development of a severe mental disorder in one of its members. Clinical impression and analytically oriented theory propose that disturbed families are much less prone to change in the structure of family organization and in the quality of interpersonal relationships than "well" families.

A number of investigators (Ackerman, 1961a; Bateson, 1956; Jackson, 1967; Lidz, 1963; Wynne *et al.*, 1958, etc.) have proposed that family interaction processes are involved in the development of the thought and behavior processes labeled as schizophrenic. Haley (1959) writes:

> A logical hypothesis about the origin of schizophrenic behavior, when the behavior is seen in communication terms, would involve the family interaction of the patient. If a child learned to relate to people in a relationship with parents who constantly induced him to respond to incongruous messages, he might learn to work out his relationships with all people in those terms. It would seem to follow that the control of the definition of relationships would be a central problem in the origin of schizophrenia (p. 332).

Ackerman (1961b) believes that "the family environment in the 'sick' families may remain essentially unaltered through the years." In such families, he writes, "The personality of the child is fixed by the time he reaches six years and thereafter changes very little . . . but if the family environment itself changes considerably over the passage of years, the ongoing interrelations . . . bring about considerable modification of the emerging personality of the child. . . ."

Other investigators, however, assume an almost reverse process. The proponents of this position, skeptical of the possible etiological role played by family behavior patterns, suggest that the patterns that are currently identified in schizophrenic families represent reactions to the illness or deviance of the child. Their position implies the assumption that family systems containing severely disturbed members undergo major changes in intrafamilial interaction processes because of the development of mental illness in one family member. They believe that comparison of current family interaction processes does not imply that family processes currently characteristic of schizophrenic families preceded and contributed to the development of the disorder.

To resolve this issue, data would have to be collected on family processes in a large sample of families, selected in a way that would increase the likelihood that at least in some families one or more members would become psychologically disturbed. Such a sample of families could be obtained from a high risk population. Stability and change in interaction patterns might then be compared in this large group of families.

EFFECTS OF OBSERVER ON "NATURAL" INTERACTION

Whenever a segment of interaction in a family, therapy, or in any other social context is selected for observation or study, the question inevitably arises as to what effects the awareness of being recorded and observed has upon the "natural" or characteristic patterns of interaction prevailing in that segment or system. This issue is so frequently raised as a criticism of systematic research on interaction contexts that it requires very serious consideration by those engaged in interaction research on family and therapy contexts. Introspection about our own behavior, in a diversity of situations and under a variety of conditions, reveals clearly enough that conditions or circumstances do, indeed, influence behavior. We sense that we and our family behave differently at the dinner table when guests are present than when they are not.

The fact that observation or study may effect some difference in interaction does not automatically invalidate (as some might assume) such efforts at observation or study. The more crucial questions concern how, in what respects, and how strongly, interaction in any given context is altered by being made the object of study or by the "presence" of an observer. Furthermore, is interactional behavior in all types of contexts (in the family, in therapy, or on a ward) equally affected by such influences?

Some systems appear to be less susceptible to modification

than other systems. Systems that have been in operation for a long time and in which individuals have experienced a myriad of similar interaction sequences seem to us to be less likely to be altered than do more recently formed systems. From this perspective it could be argued that of all interaction contexts, familial interaction contexts may perhaps be those least likely to be significantly affected by being made the subject of observation and study. This possibility remains despite the efforts of family members to conceal or disguise their interactional dynamics. The ability voluntarily to alter behavior may be a function of both periodicity (how often a sequence has been enacted) and involvement (how deeply one is invested in given sets of behavior).

A second assumption is that *content* of behavior is more susceptible to modification and to voluntary control than behavioral *process*. By process we mean, as we have indicated earlier, the sequencing and allocation of action among participants and over time. Perhaps we can illustrate this position by examining the rather intriguing proposition discussed by Haley (1962) to the effect that family behavior is affected by observation but that the behavior of so-called schizophrenic families and that of control families are differentially affected. The parents in a schizophrenic family, according to Haley, may feel more "accused and defensive" than control parents. They tend to be more guarded and "less natural." Haley's analysis, however, must follow from the assumption that there is enough "flexibility" in the interactional behaviors of members of schizophrenic families to permit them to modify their behavior in research settings in order to conceal their normal family dynamics. But to be able to change the content and form of behavior in a family implies that alternative modes of family interrelationships are available. If, however, family interaction patterns in such families are as inflexible and rigid as many clinicians and observers of such families claim, then efforts at change, made by such a family to adapt to the experimental, therapeutic, or study conditions, will not succeed.

Let us grant that family members might wish to present themselves in a more favorable light in public than they might in private. The husband might, for example, attempt to exercise greater restraint than usual in displaying his habitual response to his wife's nagging. He would then face the problem of trying to inhibit a recurrent sequence of interaction, and to introduce innovation into his responses repertory (he may treat her remarks as a jest rather than as an attack). But to the extent that his "talking back" has come to mean (for him) a defense of his vulnerable masculine status, he would have to abandon this objective along with his usual response. Less likely still would it be that family members would seek, or be able, to modify such attributes of interaction process as, for instance, rate of interchange as it prevails among members of a family.

We would expect that members of a social system would be less aware of an observer's concern with the enduring and characteristic communication patterns and process over time, and therefore we would expect least distortion in this area.

PART TWO

STUDIES IN
CLINICAL
SOCIOLOGY

Part One introduced a new theoretical framework for the study of human interaction processes and examined methods for research within that framework. Part Two reports the results and implications of some illustrative research applications of our theory and methodology.

As our data were collected largely from social contexts of interest to psychiatric or psychological clinicians, we characterize these reports as studies in clinical sociology. The data derive mainly from families with a schizophrenic youngster, a group of control families, and two sets of psychotherapy dyads, one involving therapy with neurotic outpatients and the other, therapy with hospitalized schizophrenic patients. Although we do present data that are relevant to increased understanding of family and psychotherapy interaction processes, our purpose in selecting these contexts for study did not have this objective as its primary goal. Our primary purposes were to construct and refine a research methodology applicable to the study of human interaction processes and to discover some of the more general principles governing the operation of social systems in general.

Our analysis proceeds on two levels. One deals with individuals' ideas or cognitive maps that govern the patterning of interactions involving themselves and others. These ideas, referred to by social scientists in terms of roles, rules, norms, expectations, socialization, and deutero-learning, concern what will, shall, or ought to transpire in human relationships and transactions. The second level of our analysis deals with the conceptualization, description, and analysis of behavioral action processes. At this level the focus is largely on verbal behavior, although we recognize that a comprehensive statement about human interaction processes must include other modalities of communication such as kinesic and paralinguistic phenomena as well.

One of our major theses is that social context affects the patterning of interaction in that context. Accordingly, we compared interaction patterns in different social contexts to ascertain whether there were context-related differences in interaction patterns. It will be recalled that the term social context *refers to four different ways of classifying social systems. The first three ways include comparisons between interaction patterns in (1) family versus therapy contexts, (2) German versus American family contexts, and (3) "normal" versus "disturbed" family contexts. These comparisons represent in the same order (1) the traditional sociological definition of social context in terms of a complex of interrelated roles and statuses, (2) the anthropological definition of social context in terms of social, educational, and cultural attributes, and (3) social context defined in terms of psychological attributes.*

The full recognition of the importance and implications of the fourth conception of social context, the temporal or interactional

dimension—social context as configurations of interaction—im-
pressed itself upon us only later, during the analysis of our research
findings, so we do not report any studies designed with this concep-
tion of context serving as the independent variable. It would, of
course, be quite possible and indeed desirable to proceed from this
vantage point and to compare social contexts classified in terms of
their interactional attributes rather than in terms of the more tra-
ditional typing of systems. For example, one might compare social
contexts high in interactional continuity with social contexts low in
interactional continuity, irrespective of the labels that were attached
to such contexts (family, therapy, or other).

As our analysis of interaction data progressed, it became
clear that a complex of role relationships and a psychological at-
tribute of a system member both express themselves, through time,
in the form of particular arrays of interactional patterns that unfold
as a result of the process of interaction itself. It then occurred to us
that it is the interactional attributes of human environments that
contain the "therapeutic" or "damaging" potentials of social systems, *irrespective of the combinations and permutations of role and*
psychological factors of which the systems are composed—that fam-
ilies with a schizophrenic member, for example, can be said to be
pathogenic only in so far as certain interactional structures are pres-
ent or absent in them, and that one must look at the structure of
interaction of a social system to discover its potential for a benevo-
lent outcome, rather than to classify a situation as therapeutic
merely because it involves a person aspiring to the role of therapist.

Chapter 4

Patterning of Interaction

Group and system theorists have called attention to the ways in which regularities in social interaction processes can be attributed to the duration of a group's existence. In describing such over-time characteristics of social systems, patterns have been found to be related both to the *type* of social system (problem solving group, psychotherapy group, and so on) and to the *duration* or *phase* of the interaction. For example, individuals who have met many times feel freer to discuss personal subjects than those who have interacted only once. Members of experimental problem-solving groups begin to move toward making problem-solving suggestions only after they have oriented each other as to what they think the problem is (Bales, 1950). Psychiatrists and patients explore a patient's feelings in depth only after they have made explicit the definition of the therapist-patient relationship (Lennard and Bernstein, 1960).

EFFECT OF PSYCHOLOGICAL ATTRIBUTE

Another factor that affects the patterning of interaction is the unique personalities of individual participants. Sometimes "unique" attitudes of one person toward another may accelerate or retard the evolution of relationships in a particular social group. For example, one individual might not discuss a personal matter with another, if initially he experiences mistrust for that individual. In such an instance the pattern of evolution of the relationship will bear the stamp of the particular personality and attitude of this member.

What we wish to consider now are what effects a particular *class* of psychological attributes may have on the patterning of system processes. How do particular *kinds* of psychological attributes of group members differentially affect patterning of behavior in social systems? Are the effects of such attributes, though they are made manifest through individuals, independent of the persons who exhibit them? For instance, do psychological or behavioral states described as schizophrenia, neurosis, or normality affect the patterning of interaction in groups irrespective of the unique individuals of which the groups may be composed? Does the nature of the psychological attribute itself carry certain implications for which the patterning in the over-time characteristics of the system are a function? Notice that our focus here is upon the attribute rather than upon the individual who possesses it.

The research issue that intrigues us is whether there are in social systems any characteristic interactional configurations related to the presence in those systems of members diagnosed as "schizophrenic," "neurotic," and so on. The question is whether, from an interactional frame of reference, it is possible to identify some social systems as "interactionally normal," thus a normal family system; and others as "interactionally disturbed," hence a disturbed family system? And if so, is it then possible to differentiate certain kinds of disturbed patterns as characteristically present when schizophrenia is present in a system, or neurosis; hence a "schizophrenic" social system, or a "neurotic" social system? The attractiveness of this conceptualization is that it does not foreclose upon the alternative— or at least the simultaneous possibility—that psychological attributes may sometimes themselves be the fruits of exposure to social contexts possessing certain interactional properties.

INTERACTIONAL VARIABILITY

Our expectation was that the study of interaction patterns as they unfolded in therapy systems and family systems over time might reveal some of these patterns of behavior change and might shed some light on how such changes are influenced by the psychological attributes of system members. We had available data that enabled us to compare the interaction processes in therapy systems containing a "schizophrenic" patient with the interaction processes in those containing a neurotic patient, and to compare families containing a schizophrenic member with those that did not.

Lability of emotions and instability, for instance, are psychological attributes often ascribed to so-called schizophrenics, and accordingly one might be led to expect that the interactional parameters of social systems in which such persons participated would exhibit more variability than systems composed of "normals" or "neurotics." Even among the "baffling volume of data now being produced by varied technics which study the physiology of schizophrenia . . . the fact has been established that most *measurements taken in persons suffering from this disorder are highly variable*" (Hoch, 1960, p. 206, emphasis added). We expected that an examination of the interactional patterns in systems containing a schizophrenic member would also show such instability and variability.

Up to this point, we have been able to process-analyze only a part of the data we have collected, but the findings emerging so far suggest, if anything, that social processes over time in systems containing a schizophrenic member appear to be *less* variable (are more rigid) than systems with a neurotic member. For example, as

FIGURE 2

VARIABILITY IN INTERACTION RATE

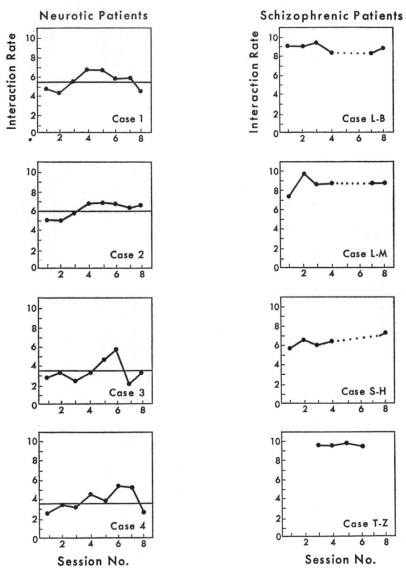

INTERACTION RATE EQUALS TOTAL NO. OF INTERACTIONS
PER SESSION DIVIDED BY NO. OF TRANSCRIBED PAGES

FIGURE 3

TRAJECTORY OF INTERACTION IN A CONTROL FAMILY

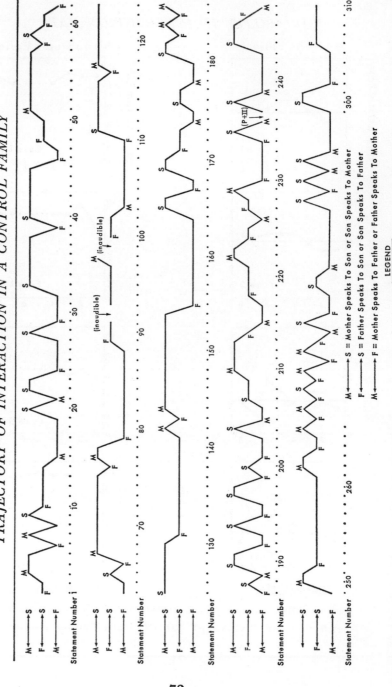

72

Figure 4

TRAJECTORY OF INTERACTION IN A "SCHIZOPHRENIC" FAMILY

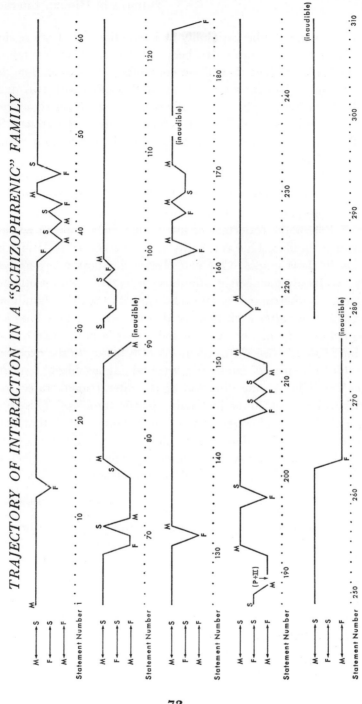

Figure 2 suggests, the variability in interaction rate from session to session of therapy appears to be much less in dyads containing a schizophrenic patient than those containing a neurotic. The deviation in the eight neurotic dyads (four therapists with two patients each) for a total of sixty-two sessions averaged 21 per cent while in the five "schizophrenic" dyads (four different therapists) for a total of twenty-five sessions, the average deviation in interaction rate was only 4 per cent.

The same kind of relative invariability can be observed in the trajectory of interaction in a family containing a schizophrenic child as compared with the trajectory in a "control" family. Figures 3 and 4 show the trajectory of interaction (who talks to whom) in two such families. One can easily trace the course of family interaction in these graphs. One can observe for how many exchanges any two family members continuously interact, when an interaction sequence is interrupted by an exchange with the other family member, and how, after each new dyad is formed, for how long it persists before it is, in turn, terminated. Long impermeable sequences of interaction between two members of a family to the exclusion of the third is typical of family triads containing a schizophrenic member. Variability in the direction of the interactional trajectory appears to be much lower in "schizophrenic families." This form of invariability is reminiscent of the "tough homeostasis" that Bateson (1959) speaks of in describing "schizophrenic" family systems and may also reflect the operation in such families of what Fleck *et al.* (1959) referred to as "narcissistic communication barriers."

PHASE DIFFERENTIATION

Differentiation of behavior over time appears to be a basic property of social systems. Psychotherapy systems (involving neurotic patients) exhibit consistent, interrelated patterns of differentiation for major dimensions of communication. Phase differentiation appears within both longer and shorter time periods (over the span of fifty sessions as well as within one session), though the actual pattern of increase or decrease for various specific communicational dimensions is not necessarily similar.

Therapy systems involving a neurotic patient were compared with those involving a schizophrenic patient with respect to the amount of communication that referred to the primary role system (role induction, socialization; see p. 146), and with respect to the amount of affective communication (references to feelings).

Figure 5 shows patterns of primary role system communication over time (the first four sessions of therapy) for eight neurotic dyads and for therapy with five schizophrenic patients upon whom

FIGURE 5

EFFECTS OF PSYCHOLOGICAL ATTRIBUTES ON PRIMARY ROLE SYSTEM COMMUNICATION

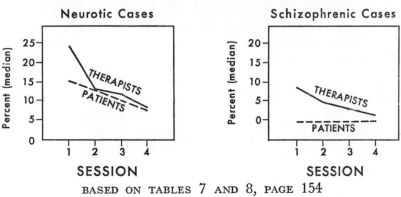

BASED ON TABLES 7 AND 8, PAGE 154

we had data available. These data are admittedly fragmentary, but they suggest that the pattern of differentiation over time that therapists exhibit so clearly among the neurotic cases appears to be attenuated in the schizophrenic cases. Schizophrenic patients emit almost no primary role system communications and appear to show no differentiation along this parameter over time.

In Figure 6, we compared the pattern of differentiation *within* the session itself by dividing each session into three phases. It can be seen that systems of therapy involving a neurotic member show a rather clear pattern of differentiation from the beginning to the end of a session, while those involving a schizophrenic tend to be more undifferentiated. For example, with neurotic patients most of a therapist's communications about the primary role system occur during the first or opening phase of the session and thence there appears to be a consistent downward trend throughout the session. The neurotic patient also shows a pattern of differentiation within the session, except that, unlike the therapist, he tends to increase his output of primary role system statements during the third or closing phase of the session. No such pattern occurs in the sessions with psychotic patients.

As to the distribution of affective communications during a therapy session, these appear to show a peak output in both types

FIGURE 6

EFFECTS OF PSYCHOLOGICAL ATTRIBUTES
ON PHASE DIFFERENTIATION

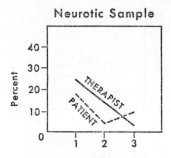

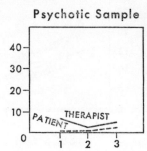

Neurotic Sample   Psychotic Sample

Phase of the session   Phase of the session
BASED ON 21 SESSIONS   BASED ON 19 SESSIONS

of system during the second or middle phase of the session, and though the difference in the *patterns* of affective communication between neurotic and schizophrenic dyads does not appear to be so great as in the primary role system dimension, the pattern is nevertheless more attenuated in the sessions with psychotics and there is considerably less affective communication in general.

We are, of course, only too well aware that these data are unfortunately very fragmentary, but we have tried to take advantage of all that we had available up to this time. Our purpose in presenting these data is mainly illustrative. We are endeavoring to introduce a perspective that directs attention to the relationship between psychological attributes and social contexts—social context not in the static sense, but in the sense of interactional configurations, distributed over time, that both change and are changed by the psychological attributes of the persons who participate in them.

Thus far we have been discussing differentiation as a *process,* a temporal or phase phenomenon, a pattern of change that occurs over a period of time; that is, over a series of meetings and over a period of an hour. But we have also previously referred to differentiation in its *structural* sense; that is, as specialization in the behavior of the participants in a social system such that different patterns of differentiation can be noted in different kinds of social *systems,* and different patterns of behavior and expectations (social roles) can be noted in different *individuals.* So far, our data have suggested, for instance, that therapy systems containing a schizophrenic patient show less differentiation in the process sense than therapy systems containing a neurotic patient. That is to say, they show less variability over time (see Figure 2). Our data also suggest that as social *systems,* systems containing schizophrenics are differentiated in the structural sense from systems that contain neurotics or normals. That is to say, they exhibit a pattern of interaction over time which is configurally or structurally different from the patterns found in the systems containing neurotics or normals (see Figures 2, 3, and 4).

What we now wish to consider is the extent to which role differentiation occurs in schizophrenic systems both in the structural sense (the extent to which each participant's behavior is differentiated from the others' behavior) and in the process sense (the extent to which the experience of interaction over time modifies the participants; that is, role-learning occurs).

Examination of the patterns of patient and therapist output of primary role system and affective statements during therapy sessions (Figure 6) shows markedly greater differentiation of patient-therapist roles in the neurotic dyads than in the schizophrenic dyads as measured by the amounts and curves of output.

EFFECT OF SOCIAL SETTING

Do attributes of individuals (psychological properties) or attributes of social contexts (sociological characteristics) have priority in determining patterns of interaction? An individual's behavior patterns that remain invariant irrespective of the role system in which he participates probably reflect the priority of psychological or personality factors. Behavior patterns that vary with the role system in which an individual participates attest to the significance of social context in influencing behavior processes.

In the preceding section we examined the effect of psychological attributes upon interaction patterns in given types of social contexts (the family and psychotherapy). The analysis of interaction data in those systems, especially of interaction process data through time, showed that the same type of social system exhibits differences along both process and structural dimensions, depending upon the psychological attributes of its members. Thus, a psychotherapy system involving a patient designated as a schizophrenic comprises a different interactional context than a psychotherapy system with a neurotic member. It therefore appears evident that one cannot assume that either the label *family* or the label *psychotherapy* necessarily identifies systems with either the same or different interactional structures or patterning, but rather that it is crucial to learn for any given problem whether it is context conceived in traditional sociological terms as a "complex of interrelated roles and statuses" or context conceived as the psychological attributes of the individuals that affects the difference in the way interaction is distributed among system participants and unfolds over time.

We had some pilot data on the behavior of the same schizophrenic patients in two different social contexts (defined in the traditional sociological sense)—with a therapist and with a parent. Thus we had available for comparison some information on the differences and the similarities in the behavior patterns of the same individuals in a patient-therapist context and in a child-parent context. Thus similarities in behavior in the two different contexts can be attributed to psychological attributes, while variability in behavior can be attributed to the differences in contexts.

We explored the variability problem first by utilizing a communicational dimension that we call "person-oriented communication" (labeling). We employ the convention of referring to person-oriented communication as Level II communication, to differentiate it from non-person-oriented communication, which we refer to as Level I communication. Level II statements are interpretations, evaluations, and identifications of the self (or other) and inner states (feelings, motives, experience, wishes).

We found the distribution of Level II communication in two different social systems in which the same patient participates to be different. In the therapy systems, the patients contributed about the same quantity of Level II statements as their therapists did; in the family systems with the same patients, they not only contributed substantially fewer Level II statements than their parents, but also reduced their own output of such statements.

The median number of Level II statements during therapy sessions was 39 for patients and 38 for therapists (based on five patients). The median number for four of the same patients with their parents was only 24, compared with 55.5 for their parents.

We also have data to indicate that in the therapy system, both patient and therapist equally are as likely to change from Level II to Level I communication as from Level I to Level II communication. However, when a patient is communicating with his parent, he inclines to change communication from Level II to Level I in each case studied while the parent moves communication in the opposite direction—from Level I to Level II. Different role settings, then, appear to generate different ratios between Level I and Level II communication, and a different dynamic of change in the exchange of such communications. In the patient-parent system we note a resistance by the patient to the continuation of Level II communication that parents persistently introduce. Thus it does appear that the context in which a patient participates makes a difference, at least with regard to this significant parameter of communication.

Contingent upon their objectives, social systems require of their members varying amounts of verbal participation. That most persons meet these requirements—which are, for the most part, implicit in different social systems—is generally taken for granted. What has not been generally accepted is that individuals diagnosed as mentally ill or as disturbed are capable of performing in accordance with differential system demands. Apparently irrespective of their psychological attributes, individuals can be sensitive to system requirements regarding verbal inputs to be contributed by each member.

We found that even for so-called schizophrenic patients verbal contributions vary with the role relationship. Patients do considerably more talking in the therapy context than in their family. The median percentage of patient propositions per transcribed page (based on thirteen sessions) was 18.9 with their therapists and only 12.9 (based on eight sessions) with their parents. The therapy relationship evidently requires a greater verbal commitment on the part of a patient than does a familial relationship, and elicits more verbalization on their part.

Though we observe a tendency for patients to accommodate their level of verbalization to that demanded by the context, the extent of their contribution may nevertheless not be sufficient to accomplish the system's objectives. In this connection we found that schizophrenic patients fail to provide minimum inputs of primary system communications during therapy. With respect to the amount of affective communication, we found that patients seem to be more willing to express feelings in a therapy context than in a family context, but the reverse is true with respect to primary system communication (see Figure 7). Family and therapy contexts then do seem to generate different rates and types of verbal outputs on the part of patients as might be expected from the different role composition and goals of these two contexts.

Not only are the quantitative and qualitative attributes of the communicational behavior of the same individuals in the two different role settings different, but so also are the characteristics of their interaction sequences in the two systems. Although we have

FIGURE 7

EFFECTS OF SOCIAL SETTING
ON PHASE DIFFERENTIATION

PATIENT-THERAPIST   PATIENT-PARENT

Primary System Communication

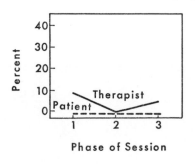
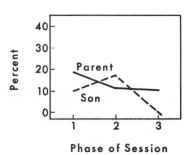

Affective Communication

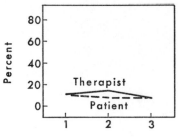
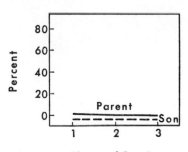

only some fragmentary data on phase differentiation in different social systems with the same schizophrenic patients, these data seem to support the proposition that the pattern of affective communications is constant over time, but with respect to primary communication in the patient-parent context, patients do appear to show a variation in the frequency of primary system references during the interaction (see Figure 7).

Context (defined in its traditional sociological sense)' thus has a twofold effect upon patterns of interaction. Different social settings affect the volume, rate, and kind of communication output, and also the vicissitudes in the interaction sequence flow over time. Our data are admittedly fragmentary in this area; they do, however, suggest some directions in which to explore the effects of social setting on interaction process.

Chapter 5

The Family Context

~~~~~~

Social behavior is governed by socially shared principles; consequently, it is possible, through observation of individuals in social interaction, to make inferences regarding the principles governing such behavior. Many such principles apply to given systems of interaction and behavior irrespective of the particular social context in which the individuals are interacting. Verbal interactions exhibit certain uniformities attributable to the operation of culturally learned and shared principles. For example, one set of principles pertains to language behavior. One such, easily observable, uniformity relating to language behavior is that individuals are supposed to speak not at the same time but sequentially; another is that a certain change in inflection connotes a question; and still another is that a question is (usually) intended to solicit an answer.

NORMS AND METANORMS IN FAMILIES

Principles that govern interpersonal behavior are referred to as *norms* by sociologists. Social norms are conceived of as ideas or paradigms describing ranges of behavior and attitudes that are appropriate or inappropriate in given social contexts. *Role* and *role behavior* refer to uniformities in behavior and attitude between occupants of reciprocal status positions (teacher-student, father-son, salesman-customer) which derive from the sets of social norms governing these relationships.

Individuals are generally unaware of norms while they are interacting because the demands of the interaction process are so complex that awareness of the principles or norms involved in specific role relationships and contexts would be dysfunctional. Maintaining total awareness of social norms during interaction is analogous to thinking about principles of grammar and syntax while trying to carry on a conversation.

That individuals in interaction can remain unaware of the principles guiding their behavior has been explained as dependent upon the "complementarity" of social norms. As Spiegel (1957) writes:

> The principle of complementarity is of the greatest significance because it is chiefly responsible for that degree of harmony and stability which occurs in interpersonal relations. Because so many of the roles in which any of us are involved are triggered off by cultural cues in a completely complementary fashion, we tend not to be aware of them. We enact them automatically, and all goes well. This automatic function of role systems has significance for psychological economy of effort. We are spared the necessity of coming to decisions about most of the acts we perform because we know our parts so well (pp. 3–4).

Only when complementarity fails and the limits of a social

norm are violated may there emerge, along with a sense of transgression, an awareness of the norm that has been transgressed.

A social norm may be said to be "institutionalized" in a particular group if a large number of members of the group accept it, adhere to it, and impose sanctions on group members who fail to conform to it. Such sanctions range from inducing a sense of discomfort in the transgressor to expelling him from the group. Individuals vary in the extent to which they adhere to given norms and perceive as a transgression others' non-adherence to a given norm.

In his original version of "Study of the Family," Jackson (1965) writes:

> . . . a theory which described the family as a system organized around *rules* might prove to be most useful. Such a theory might help to account for the recurrent patterns which we have already observed in our study of families.

Moreover, he writes, it "appears vital to efficiency that norms be covert and institutionalized." But Jackson does not believe that at present we need to be concerned with how a particular family derives its norms and values; that is to say, whether from the culture or from unique experiences in their families of origin. Nevertheless, there are at least three kinds of family norms, representing three different origins. There are those general norms that govern certain interactions in a family to the same extent that they govern those kinds of interactions in other contexts (for example, norms relating to language behavior and gesture). Parents are mainly responsible for the induction of children into such norm-appropriate behavior. When performing this task, parents function as the representatives of society as a whole.

The very generality and pervasiveness of such norms are responsible in large measure for the ordering of human relationships. An absorbing interest in the study of family interaction should not blind one to the derivative quality of most of the behavior that occurs in any given social context. While the source of such norms derives from the society or culture, one should also bear in mind that subcultures of a regional, ethnic, economic, and religious kind also give rise to qualitatively different versions of some of the more general social norms.

We can distinguish, in addition to norms that operate in all social systems, a second set of norms that concern only *particular* social systems, for example, the family. Consider only a few such norms—those governing family residence, sleeping arrangements, allocation of protective and work functions among parents and children, and differential restraints upon sexuality.

Third, there are norms that evolve idiosyncratically within each family in the course of its working out its own special relationship problems. It is primarily to these norms that Jackson's concept of "family rules" seems to refer. A most important characteristic of this class of norms is that they usually embody qualifications, modifications, or redefinitions of one of the more general family norms.

To account for such self-generated family norms requires us to hypothesize the existence of some higher order principles, which might be termed *metanorms*. Metanorms would refer to rules that govern norms, their implementation, modification, and redefinition. Just as norms, in general, can be considered to have evolved to regulate the relation of persons in society in such a way as to provide order, cooperation, and task fulfillment, so can it be argued that special rules evolve whenever family systems are threatened by conflict or disintegration. But every new set of rules that are generated implies the application of other rules—rules about rules. We have called these rules about rules metanorms.

When identifying a family rule, then, an observer faces a three-fold task: (1) to specify the general family norm that is involved, (2) to describe the nature of the modification of the norm that occurs in the particular family, and (3) to identify the metanorm that justifies that modification. A rule like "No one in this family listens or responds to anyone else," which may appear to operate in a particular family, makes sense only when one recognizes that this rule modifies or runs counter to the more generally prescribed and sanctioned norm that individuals in face-to-face contact listen and respond to each other, and that this modification results from the invocation of a metanorm when the application of the general norm would be dysfunctional for some family members or threaten the family system.

Familial interaction may be subject to strain whenever there is a "lack of fit" between the requirements of family life and the attributes and capabilities of the individual family members comprising the system. Vulnerability to strain on the part of individual members of a family can also be assumed to result from their earlier interactional history which is internalized in the personality structure.

From this it would follow, as Jackson points out, that rules represent homeostatic mechanisms that tend to reduce family strain. Thus, few families would require rules were family system requirements and individual attributes and capabilities articulated well with each other. In healthy, satisfied families we would expect to see in operation many norms, but few "rules." While in disturbed or discordant families we would anticipate the appearance of many "idiosyncratic norms" or "rules" resulting from the application of metanorms that justify their adoption. The process can be compared to that observed in groups who are unable to cooperate in the fulfillment of their assigned task and who consequently devote considerable time to the development of *procedural* rules on how to move ahead with the task.

Rules are not adhered to nor subscribed to with the same conviction by every member of a family. Rules probably revolve around family members who present the most severe strain to the system; that is to say, those for whom there is the least fit between capabilities (personality) and system demands.

The evolution and application of metanorms in a social system should not in itself be viewed as a negative feature of social systems, although they are seen as "indicators" of system strain in family systems. At a later point in this book we shall discuss the function of metanorms in relation to *transitional contexts* such as the psychotherapy context in which metanorms are frequently employed both as a means for developing the psychotherapy system and of redefining social contexts for the patient.

HARMONY AND DISCORDANCE IN FAMILY SYSTEMS

A common observation about interaction patterns in social systems is that they may be harmonious or discordant. Some groups are torn by disagreement while others are high on consensus and agreement. Expectational complementarity among group members tends to stabilize and preserve social systems, while lack of complementarity and disagreement should tend to disintegrate them.

It seemed to us that an examination of the number of agreements and disagreements that actually occur between participants interacting in different social contexts might provide data on the extent to which diverse social contexts generate differences in the patterning of interaction processes. At the same time, we also considered it useful to compare configurations of agreement and disagreement for groups having different characteristics (for example, families with and without patient members).

Interactions in three types of social contexts are available for comparison: families, therapeutic discussion groups, and problem-solving groups in a laboratory setting. Comparisons were possible *within* contexts by comparing the interaction pattern of a "most satisfied" laboratory group with that of a "least satisfied" laboratory group, and the interaction pattern of "disturbed" families (those containing a schizophrenic child) with that of "non-disturbed" families (those with no identified problem). The findings are summarized in Table 1.

Proceeding from Bales' (1953) observation that "positive reactions are usually more numerous than negative reactions and that one would intuitively feel that any group process would be self-defeating and self-limiting were the negative reaction to predominate (p. 117)," we computed a ratio of concordance for each type of group. By dividing the percentage of group agreements by the percentage of group disagreements, we computed an agreement/disagreement ratio such that a ratio of 1.00 indicated an equal number of agreements and disagreements. The higher the ratio, the greater the concordance in the group.

As expected, the concordance ratio in Bales' "most satis-

Table 1

PATTERNS OF AGREEMENT*

	Average % Agreement	Average % Disagreement	Ratio of Concordance
Bales' "Most Satisfied Group"[a]	24.9	4.0	6.22
Therapeutic Groups[b]	4.8	1.8	2.70
"Typical Laboratory Groups"[b]	16.5	7.8	2.11
Control Families[c]	11.8	10.9	1.05
Bales' "Least Satisfied Group"[a]	9.6	12.4	.77
"Schizophrenic" Families[c]	8.6	13.8	.61

* Categorization of agreement and disagreement is based on Bales' interaction process coding and a corresponding set of categories developed by Lennard. For a full description of agreement-disagreement coding of family data see pp. 113–128 of this book. Disagreement, for example, includes rejection, contradiction, scepticism, sarcasm.
   [a] Taken from Table 1, Bales, 1953, p. 116.
   [b] Taken from Table 2, Talland, 1955, p. 461.
   [c] For description of the selection of families see pp. 95–96.

fied" of sixteen laboratory groups was found to be higher than the concordance ratio in Bales' "least satisfied" of the sixteen groups (6.22 vs. .77). In fact, these two groups attained almost the highest and the lowest concordance of any of the groups upon which we had data, thus suggesting a reasonable relationship between group satisfaction and concordance.

Using definitions of agreement and disagreement similar to those embodied in the Bales' categories, we analyzed verbal interaction in eighteen families (see pp. 113–120). Ten of the families were families containing a schizophrenic child and eight were control families (families with no identified problem). The concordance ratios computed for the families containing a schizophrenic child ranged from a low of 0.20 to a high of 1.7 with a mean of 0.61, while for the eight control families the concordance ratio was only slightly higher, ranging from a low of 0.55 to a high of 3.0 with a mean of 1.05. *Twelve of the eighteen families exhibited a concordance ratio of 1.0 or below.*

That concordance in "disturbed" families is likely to be lower than in "control" families comes as no surprise and interestingly parallels the difference we observed between Bales' "most satisfied" and "least satisfied" groups. But what was unanticipated was the finding that concordance in family systems as a whole seems lower than in *any* of the other social contexts we examined. Avererage concordance in the families observed seems to be closer to the magnitude of Bales' "least satisfied" groups than to the magnitude of concordance in any of the other contexts. The average concordance ratio in our sample of families was only *half as high* as in the typical laboratory groups and only about *one-sixth* as high as in the Bales' most satisfied group (see Table 1).

It should be kept in mind that the quantitative data that we have assembled on concordance in diverse social contexts was based on small samples gathered for limited periods of interaction and under a variety of conditions. Yet the data seem to suggest that social contexts do generate differential frequencies and ratios of communicative acts expressing conflict and discordance. More specifically, it appears that the family context (studied in a laboratory setting) generates more discordance and disagreement than do *ad hoc* laboratory groups or other special purpose systems such as psychotherapy. One would suspect that the ratio of concordance might be still lower in "natural" family interaction. It appears to us that the relative prevalence of "positive" and "negative" communications generated by different social contexts deserves considerable further exploration and analysis.

Assuming that our finding about the tendency of the family context to generate low concordance patterns is a valid one and not an artifact of sampling or of the research design and laboratory context in which the data were gathered, we could address ourselves to some of the implications of that finding and to a discussion of the properties of the family system that might account for its tendency to create conflict.

The family is the most enduring and permanent of all the

social subsystems that have been studied and perhaps the most enduring of all social configurations. Even though there has been speculation about the possible disintegration of the family as an institution, it is still less vulnerable to "breakup" than other social groups, such as psychotherapy groups or work groups. A family has both a longer history and a longer life expectancy than any of the other contexts of social interaction. Thus the constraints against the expression of disagreement that may operate in other, less stable contexts are not needed in the family context for the preservation of the system. Perhaps the expectation of acceptance, as well as the awareness of the more limited options available, allows family members to "be themselves" more openly than do other groups, and thus differences are more openly revealed. Moreover, because of the enduring nature of family relationships, concealment of differences by a family member involves a continuing problem and a much greater commitment than does such concealment in more temporary statuses. For example, concealing food preferences and dislikes from friends during a weekend visit is easier than concealing them from one's own family over a period of years. This does not mean that *all* differences are revealed in family life. For as has been pointed out by investigators such as Ackerman (1958), Jackson (1965), Wynne (1958) and others, family members may "conspire" or "agree" to conceal or repress differences and disagreement.

The character of family life is such that the degree of affective involvement on the part of its members is probably more intense than in other social systems. This issue is further complicated by the fact that, unlike most other systems, the family includes members of different generational statuses. Social contexts containing members who are of different ages and generational statuses are likely to have more problems in establishing consensus than those that are more homogeneous in composition. For all of these reasons, there is an inherent plausibility to the finding that family contexts would elicit a differential distribution of communications, along an agreement/disagreement axis.

Some thought might now be devoted to the effect on family members of consistent exposure to particular configurational characteristics. As Bales (1953) has suggested, certain balances between types of communication are required to move group interaction process forward toward the accomplishment of the tasks the group has undertaken. He therefore maintains that positive reactions (agreements) must outnumber negative reactions (disagreements) and that answers must be more numerous than questions. This conception of an optimal balance among significant parameters of communication in an adequately functioning system is most intriguing, and it deserves more attention.

If imbalance among given parameters of communication is dysfunctional for the achievement of system goals, then exposure to imbalanced communicational configurations (for example, low concordance) might be dysfunctional for individual group members as well. One may assume that individuals vary in their ability to tolerate conflict within a family context, whether or not they themselves are the target of such behaviors. Individuals may have differential thresholds for coping with disagreements (such as negative evaluation, contradiction, disconfirmation) within their interactional environments.

Such thresholds can be conceived of as limits on the ability to process and neutralize given amounts of disorienting, disorganizing, and damaging communication present in an interactional context. Such limits vary among individuals, probably depending upon their exposure to previous interactional configurations. Symptoms of psychological disturbance then might be conceived as ways of dealing with interactional fields—for example, withdrawal from interpersonal contacts involving extreme communicational imbalance.

The notion of communicational configurations makes it possible to view the removal of an individual from the family context into other contexts (defined as therapeutic) in a different light. What may be significant about the "therapeutic" context may be conceived of as a change in the interactional configurations and balances that prevail in the new context.

Exposure to what might appear to be only a slight difference in the occurrence of some kinds of communications and in their configurations (for example, agreement/disagreement ratio) may be significant in that, in the new context, thresholds are not exceeded and given kinds of communications remain within tolerance limits, so that an individual is not strained beyond his ability to process them.

PATTERNS IN TWO TYPES OF FAMILIES

Clinicians have called attention to certain distinctive features of intrafamilial interaction processes in families containing a schizophrenic member. Descriptions of such families by Ackerman (1961a), Bateson (1956), Bowen (1959), Goldfarb *et al.* (1961), Jackson (1959), Lidz (1963), Wynne and Singer (1965), and many others are important sources of hypotheses on how such families differ from others, and how family interaction may contribute to the development or maintenance of a so-called schizophrenic disorder in a family member. We are certain that these investigators would agree that their hypotheses deserve further specification and more systematic research documentation.

Our purpose here is to attempt to provide such research documentation by comparing interaction patterns in a group of families containing a child diagnosed as schizophrenic with a group of control families, with respect to the kinds and sequences of communication, utilizing quantitative methods for the study of such family processes.

One way to study the family and the effect that the family may have upon each of its members is to view the structure and patterns of interaction that prevail among the family members as comprising an interactional context, or environment, within which family members must function. This perspective requires a shift in the focus of attention from the characteristics of the individual members of a family, to the properties of the relationships that characterize their interactions. Relationships and interaction patterns can be conceived of as system elements which exhibit definable order, interdependence and variation.

We have suggested elsewhere (see System Properties of Social Systems, Chapter One) that some variation may occur among the variables constituting a system and yet the system can retain its identity and accomplish the goals for which it has been assembled, unless it is characterized by either excessive rigidity or excessive instability in its parameters, which would indicate a disturbance in some system function. Such disturbances may occur if one or all of the participants in a social system do not contribute the requisite amounts of the required informational and emotional inputs. Systems may fail if one or more members are not permitted to interact or if they fail to maintain appropriate interactional levels.

We undertook to identity significant patterns of family interactional contexts, and to relate these patterns to individual and family "outcomes." Our assumption is that families characterized by particular interactional configurations or by the presence or absence of specific system properties and mechanisms exercise different effects on family members.

Some of the variables we selected for systematic examination derive from a theoretical model of the family as constituting a small communication system. In this section we are mainly concerned with the amount, rate, and direction of intrafamily communication and the availability and strength of communication channels among family members. Other variables are derived from an analysis of the family as a regulation and control system that determines the appropriateness, direction, and rate of behavior of its members. Of special interest is communication that is self-initiated, especially the frequency with which a third member of a family trialogue attempts to intrude into an ongoing dialogue between two other family members. We shall study the encouragement or discouragement of intrusions, for they are considered to be a significant parameter in the unfolding of family interaction process.

We are also concerned with the study of each family's allocation of action among its members and over time. More specifically, we determine the extent to which a family succeeds in the formation and dissolution of subsystems and in the maintenance of interactional continuity within the subsystems (dyads) formed.

Another set of dimensions follows from the recognition of "confirmation" as one of the significant characteristics of human interaction. We assess the frequencies and types of agreement and disagreement generated in family contexts and note the balance between agreement and disagreement characteristic of the communicational environment evolved by the family as a whole. Last, but by no means least, the family may be viewed as a socialization system that concerns itself with, among its other functions, enabling children to identify and articulate inner states. Here we are concerned with how parents elicit and respond to the motives and feelings of their children. Of particular interest are the frequency and the character of parental communications in which the child's experiences, motives, and feelings are interpreted. A focus on homeostatic system processes is here linked up with family socialization behavior.

Since we are well aware of the heterogeneous and unselected character of our samples, with respect to both the schizophrenic group as well as the control group, it is realistic to expect within the groups considerable variability in the types and sequences of communication that we are quantifying. But the kind of comparisons we are attempting to make should, nonetheless, permit a kind of gross assessment as to whether any of the patterns are distinctly more prevalent within the disturbed family group than in the control group.

The group of "schizophrenic" families consisted of ten families in which a son had been diagnosed as schizophrenic, borderline schizophrenic, or psychotic. Rather than repeat the cumbersome phrase, "families with a child diagnosed as schizophrenic" we shall use the briefer expression, "schizophrenic families" throughout. We attach no diagnostic implication to this convention. The diagnoses for seven of the children were made at the Child Guidance Clinic of Kings County Hospital in New York City; for two, at the New York State Psychiatric Institute; and for one at Rockland State Hospital. Although it was not feasible for our staff to review the diagnoses, descriptions in the case records did suggest that the sample included very highly disturbed children. Nevertheless, the patients may well have constituted a heterogeneous group of psychological disorders. For example, the record of one child contains descriptive phrases such as "fragile ego," "identity problem," "isolation of affect," "paranoid fears," and so on. In another record, we find descriptive phrases such as "borderline case with fluidity of

ego boundaries with possible schizophrenic and dissociative tendencies." Questions dealing with the validity and reliability of psychiatric classification and diagnosis are briefly alluded to elsewhere
(see Social Setting and Behavior, Chapter Two), but in the main
lie outside the scope of our book.

All the patients were males between nine and fourteen years
of age who came from working-class, Jewish families with at least
one other sibling.

Each sample of family interaction was obtained from a
forty-five-minute discussion among father, mother, and son. While
it may be argued that a discussion among all members of the family
would provide a more accurate representation of family process, we
were inclined toward Bowen's (1960) view that the primary family
members involved in the family conflict are the father, the mother,
and the patient, and that, in effect, father, mother, and the identified patient form the family group of most interest for study. Moreover, since the consequence of differences in the number of members
of a family upon the patterns of intrafamily communication is un-
determined, it seemed wiser to control for family size at this ex-
ploratory stage of research.

The seven control families were volunteers recruited from a
public housing project located near Kings County Hospital. Families eligible to reside in this project were limited to an annual income of $7,000. The cooperation of the families was enlisted by a
member of the project's housing committee, who contacted families
who met the study criteria and offered ten dollars as payment for
participation. A screening interview was conducted with each child
in the control group by a psychiatrist to ascertain that there was no
apparent major psychological disturbance.

The families were taken to the one-way vision screen room
by one of the investigators, who explained that they would be asked
to discuss three topics for fifteen minutes each, and that at the end
of each fifteen-minute period, the investigator would return to learn
what they had concluded, as well as to assign them a new topic.
They were also told that their conversation was to be recorded. The
topics for discussion were: (1) Would you discuss whether or not

a boy might have some duties to perform around the house, and, if so, what they might be? (2) When a boy needs a helping hand with his homework, do you think it is better for mother or for father to help out? (3) Here is a list of jobs that a boy might think of doing later in life (typed on a card): fireman, teacher, reporter, dentist, pilot, and engineer. Would you discuss these occupations among yourselves and list, in order, the three you think best. These topics are formulated on a level that permits their discussion by a child of nine, and they also require the participation of all three family members.

All of the sessions were tape-recorded and subsequently transcribed verbatim. Each individual's statements appeared in the transcript in the sequence in which it occurred, the typist taking special note of all instances in which one family member interrupted another family member. Each statement in the verbatim transcript of a session was coded along a variety of dimensions— for example, who originated the statement, toward whom the statement was directed, the category of implicit and explicit agreement and disagreement. The statement was selected as the unit of analysis for coding purposes. A statement provides a unit that is both manageable (for IBM analysis) and "natural," in the sense that it involves a minimum of arbitrariness in delineating a unit.

Using the statement as a basic unit makes it possible to combine statements in a number of ways for comparative purposes. For example, it is possible to compare within any session the differential frequency of given types of communications by each family member over specified time intervals and to compare the communication patterns of one family member with that of the other two family members. On another level of analysis, it is possible to compare the communication pattern of a particular status in the family (for example, son) with the communication pattern of the same status in the other families, either control or schizophrenic. These comparisons can be made for the session as a whole, or between specified time intervals within a session. On still another level, it is possible to compare the patterns of communication in the "schizophrenic" families with the control families as a whole.

Figure 8

FAMILY PATTERNS: VOLUME OF COMMUNICATION

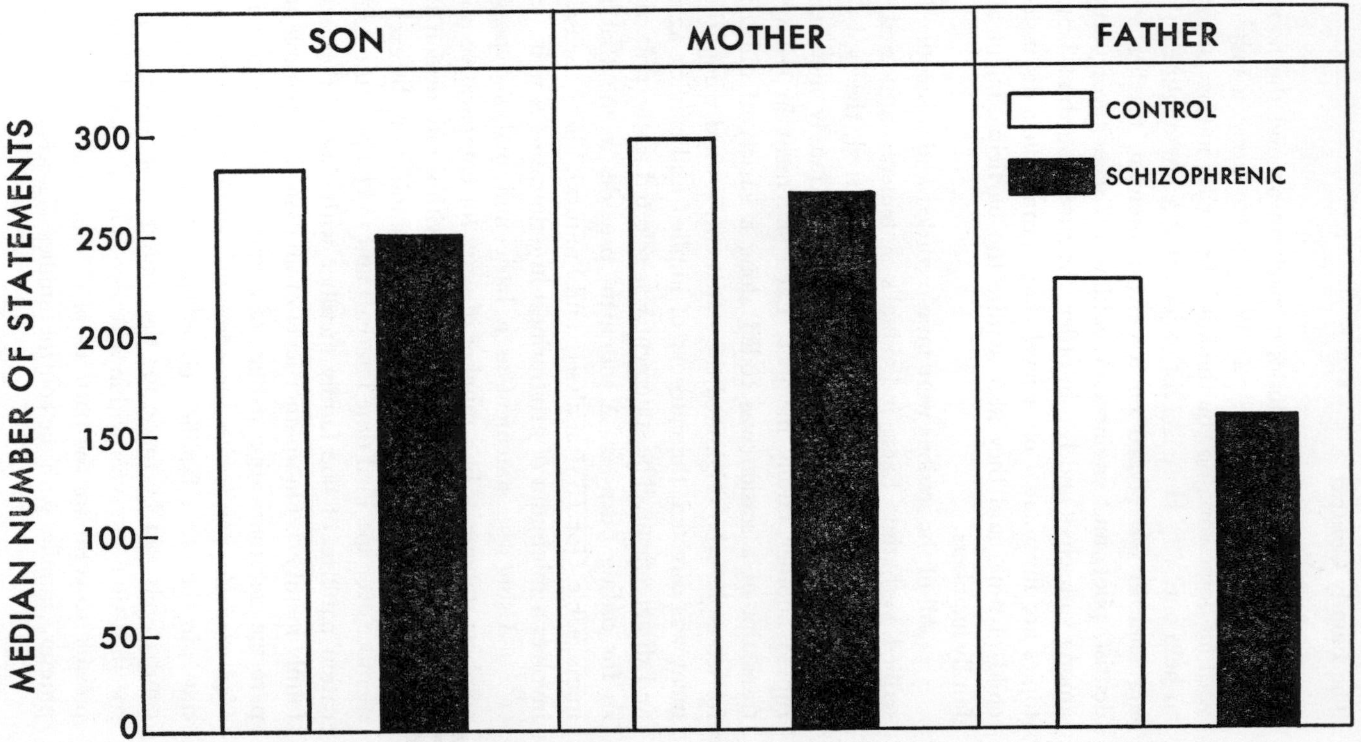

First we wished to ascertain whether the total volume of communication and its distribution among family members were significantly different in the two groups.

Figure 8 shows that there are no conspicuous differences between the "schizophrenic" and the control families in the median number of statements made during the discussion period. But although the sons and mothers in the "schizophrenic" families emit almost the same number of statements as their counterparts in the control families, the median number of communications by the fathers in the "schizophrenic" families was found to be lower.

In a study involving a small number of families in each group, when sample homogeneity is doubtful, the median appears to be a better measure of trends than the mean. However, means are presented whenever median and mean are close.

CHANNELS OF COMMUNICATION

Epstein and Westley (1959) postulate that "communication among the members is necessary to the successful functioning of the family . . . it should be obvious that needs cannot be satisfied, problems solved, or goals reached without communication (p. 1)." To the extent that the fulfillment of a group's goals and the satisfaction of its members depend upon communication among group members, the group's effectiveness will depend upon whether the members of the group feel free and are able to communicate with each other. The ability to communicate within a system is ultimately dependent upon the availability of channels of communication within that system. Without such channels of communication, transmission of information is impossible.

In a triadic group consisting of a father, mother, and son, there are three bidirectional channels of communication: (1) father-son; (2) mother-son; and (3) father-mother. Hence, there are six directions in which communications can flow. In Figure 9, we have charted the direction of flow and the utilization of the six channels of communication in our "schizophrenic" and control families.

It can be seen that the *configuration* of communication flow is markedly different in the group of "schizophrenic" families than in the group of control families. In the "schizophrenic" families, the son addresses significantly fewer (at the .025 level)* communications to the father and also receives fewer communications from him than in the control families; thus, the father-son channel is underutilized. The father-mother channel of communication also appears to be grossly underutilized. In contrast, the mother directs more communications to the son and receives more from him in the "schizophrenic" families than in the control families.

There appears to be a consistently lower utilization of four of the channels of communication in the "schizophrenic" family system, all of which involve communications with the father. These findings correspond very closely to the description by Fleck *et al.* (1959), and others, of the "unusual passivity" of the fathers of schizophrenics. Our findings also bring to mind Epstein and Westley's (1959) hypothesis that "when a parent is the focus of such impaired communication, it is an indication that he or she is a source of pathological disturbance in family functioning (p. 7)."

To a certain extent, the proportion of communications flowing to and from each of the participants in a family system reflects the saliency of the participant, or his status, in that system. Thus, one might conclude that all three family role relationships appear to have somewhat more equal salience in the control families than they have in the "schizophrenic" families; while in the "schizophrenic" families, the mother-son role relationship seems to be dominant. These differences lend support to Lidz's (1963) statement to the effect that one problem to avoid in small groups, including the family, is the formation of subgroups or dyadic coalitions, in order that the participants remain open to multiple communication and affiliation. Our data seem to confirm the clinical hypothesis that in many "schizophrenic" families in which the identified patient is a male, one dyadic unit (mother-son) operates to the exclusion of the other family role relationships.

It seems reasonable to suppose that for adequate family

* Mann-Whitney Test. See Siegel (1956).

Figure 9

FAMILY PATTERNS: CHANNELS OF COMMUNICATION

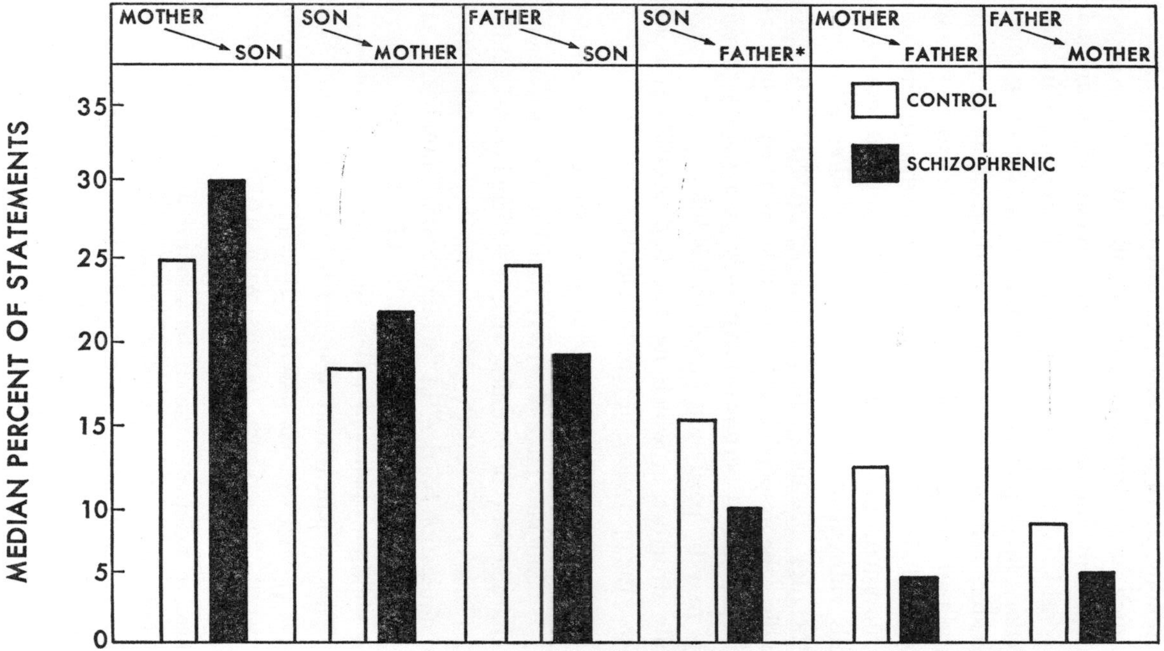

*Significant at .025 (Mann-Whitney)

functioning, all of the possible family role relationships must obtain, as much as all statuses in the family must be occupied. Broken families and families in which role relationships are defective can be considered to be inadequately differentiated in structure and function. Inadequate family differentiation may be correlated with individual differentiation and is, perhaps, both in the present and in the past, responsible for the latter. Role-learning occurs, as Parsons and Bales (1955) imply, both through participation in a family subsystem and also through observing the operation of other family subsystems. Deficits in communication between father and mother, for example, lessen a child's opportunity to learn or to internalize the respective role statuses involved. The inability of a schizophrenic to perform adequately in a variety of role relationships may be partly attributed to his having been raised within a family structure in which he has had insufficient opportunity to observe the operations of family role relationships.

INITIATION AND CONTROL OF INTERACTION

Clinicians have observed that certain phenomena appear to be characteristic of families with a schizophrenic child. For example, Fleck *et al.* (1959) refer to what they call "the narcissistic communication barrier" in "schizophrenic" families. "Certain mothers—or fathers—are quite incapable of responding spontaneously to their children's behavior unless the parent has evoked such behavior. Thus, a parent may respond to a young child's behavior only if it is elicited by that parent." Bruch (1962a) also observes that the word "impervious" occurs with striking frequency in studies describing schizophrenic families. She regards it as important to determine whether a given behavioral act should be regarded as an "initiation" or a "response." This notion of initiated communication versus responsive communication is reminiscent of Skinner's (1938) distinction between operant and respondent behavior.*

In two pilot studies, with very small samples,** we found

* A speculative, though intriguing, notion is offered by Bateson (in a personal communication), who sees in the mode of current handling of a child's effort to "enter" familial interaction a reflection and a repetition of the original intrusion of the child at birth into the parental relationship.

** Using data made available at the Department of Psychiatry of that identified schizophrenic patients had very little success in "intruding" into mother-father interactions. In this connection, one could speak of "permeability" or "lack of permeability" in the dyadic interactions or the coalitions that form during family interaction depending upon the ease with which a third member can intrude himself into an ongoing dyadic communication sequence. One question raised by this pilot work was whether the lack of response to intrusion and the lack of permeability were due to unresponsiveness on the part of the parents, or to the strength of the bond between the parents that excluded the child. Our present finding with respect to the deficit in communication between father and mother in "schizophrenic" families tends to support the former hypothesis.

The transition from childhood to healthy adulthood requires acquisition of the capacity for self-initiated or autonomous behavior.* As in any social system, participation in a family system places constraints upon the rate, direction, and type of behavior permitted among its members. Moreover, each family tends to develop and maintain its own definitions about how much and what kind of behavior is permissible during family interactions, though these definitions are supposed to be subject to revision when changes take place in the statuses of the family members (see Norms and Metanorms at the beginning of this chapter). Of great interest, then, would be an examination of the way in which different kinds of families deal with the occurrence of children's efforts at self-initiated behavior. Children's efforts to gain their parents' attention or to redirect parental dialogues represent a frequent and typical form of self-initiated behavior. Such instances of intrusion provide a readily quantifiable indicator of the way in which families reinforce, control, and allocate the initiation of communication. Each such entry by a third person into a two-person interaction, which

---

the Jewish Family Service (in collaboration with N. W. Ackerman) and data made available by Frances Cheek.

* The significance of this parameter is stressed by Bettelheim, who states that his work demonstrates "how important it is that from birth on the child gets responses from the environment that encourage his spontaneous moves toward the world; he should not be ignored or overpowered" (*New York Times Magazine,* Jan. 12, 1967).

is not requested or elicited by the persons in interaction, can be called an *intrusion*. We can then construct measures of the frequency, success, and duration of the effect of such intrusions for each member of our sample of families; and we can determine, for each family member, the number of times he initiates efforts to intervene, the number of times he succeeds in becoming part of an ongoing interaction between two other family members, and with what success his efforts meet.

By focusing on any pair of family members who are intruded upon, one can determine how responsive or impervious they are to intrusions by a third family member, especially how permissive parents are of intrusions by their child. One can also assess the rates and types of intrusions characteristic of a given family as an indicator of the family's toleration and encouragement of self-initiated behavior, and can compare data on schizophrenic and control families with respect to these parameters.

For the purpose of coding, a statement is categorized as an *intrusion attempt* if (1) the person making the statement is neither the target nor the initiator of the previous exchange; and (2) the previous exchange involves the other two persons in the triad. An exchange is defined as a sequence of two statements during which ego directs a communication to alter, and alter responds with a communication to ego. An intrusion may be regarded as successful only if it yields at least one communication directed to the "intruder" by either of the interactors. An indicator of the *degree* of the success of an intrusion is the number of interactions that it yields. Thus, an intrusion that results in four exchanges with the "intruder" is more successful than one that results in only two exchanges. An unsuccessful intrusion is one that does not result in any exchange with the "intruder," but rather, leaves the ongoing interaction continuing uninterrupted.

Figure 10 compares the median number of intrusion attempts that occur in seven control and ten schizophrenic families.

It can be seen that considerably fewer intrusion attempts occur in the "schizophrenic" families than in the control families. It is particularly clear that the mothers and the sons in the "schizo-

FIGURE 10

FAMILY PATTERNS: FREQUENCY OF
INTRUSION ATTEMPTS

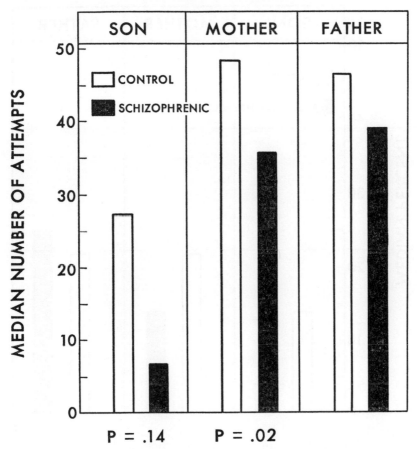

phrenic" families attempt considerably fewer intrusions than the mothers and sons in the control families. In addition to the difference in the absolute number of intrusion attempts, it also appears (see Figure 11) that the *proportion* of the mothers' and sons' statements that are attempted intrusions is lower in the schizophrenic than in the control families.

Since the absolute number of intrusion attempts may reflect

FIGURE 11

FAMILY PATTERNS: PERCENT OF
INTRUSION ATTEMPTS

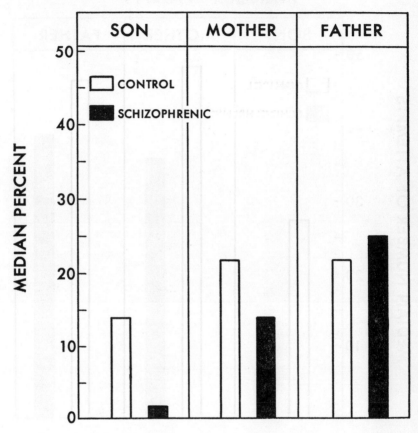

simply different total amounts of interaction, and fewer exchanges
between any two family members upon whom to intrude (for example, see Figure 9, the deficit of interaction between mother and
father in "schizophrenic" families), the data were reanalyzed to
control for the number of "opportunities" to intrude. We computed
the ratio between the number of intrusion attempts and the total
number of intrusion opportunities (for example, total number of
exchanges between mother and father divided by the number of

intrusion attempts by son). Figure 12 shows that the ratio of intrusion attempts by patient-sons is lower than that by sons in control
families.

FIGURE 12

*FAMILY PATTERNS: INTRUSION ATTEMPTS OVER
INTRUSION OPPORTUNITIES*

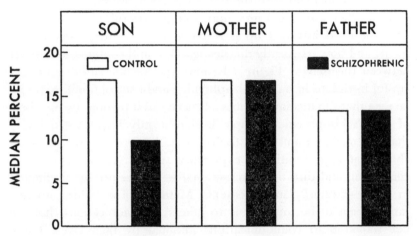

It appears that a deficit in self-initiated behavior (as measured by intrusion rates) is characteristic of the patient-son status
in "schizophrenic" families. This is reflected in the extremely low
absolute number of intrusion attempts, the proportionately lower
number of intrusion attempts, and the lower ratio of intrusion attempts to intrusion opportunities. Since our data (see Figure 8) do
not show any significantly lower participation and volume of activity by our patients, this finding regarding lower intrusion rates
cannot be considered to be an artifact of the generally lower activity
level that is commonly thought to be characteristic of the schizophrenic disorder. Rather, it seems to us that the differences in the
intrusion patterns reflect the way in which "schizophrenic" families regulate and inhibit certain types of behavior.

It will be recalled that the parents of schizophrenic patients
are believed to discourage those forms of behavior for which Bruch's

(1962a) term *initiating* seems appropriate—behavior in which the child redirects the focus and content of communication. The discouragement or nonreinforcement of self-initiated behavior should certainly be expected to lead to its reduction or extinction over time. We hypothesize that the reduced intrusion rates that we found reflect the product of this process.

To test the hypothesis that self-initiated behavior receives less reinforcement in "schizophrenic" families, we analyzed the degree to which attempted intrusions were successful. How frequently does the dyad intruded upon respond to the third person's statement; and how frequently do they ignore it and continue to interact between themselves? Figure 13 shows the median number of successful intrusions in our "schizophrenic" and control families. It can be seen that the median number of successful intrusions by members of our "schizophrenic" sample is significantly lower (.025 level) than the median number for the controls. Accordingly, we may conclude that opportunities to experience success (reinforcement) in controlling and directing interactional sequences are highly limited in "schizophrenic" family contexts. Members of a "schizophrenic" family seem to be impervious to others' communications that are not responses to communications initiated by themselves. Laing (1962) says that "The other who is felt to be unresponsive or impervious to the self as agent, or is *in fact* unresponsive, tends to induce by this imperviousness a sense of emptiness and impotence in the self (p. 72)."

CONTINUITY OF INTERACTION

In order for family members to accomplish any of a family's numerous functions and tasks, they must engage in interactional sequences that continue for some "optimal" period. Indeed, relationships can be evolved and problems can be resolved only if there is some continuity of interaction among the persons involved.

Themes and issues, however, exhibit a tendency toward closure and termination. There are natural topical discontinuities in conversation; having exhausted one topic, one moves on to the next. Some interactions may be completed after one exchange, others require longer sequences of exchanges. Interactional sequences

FIGURE 13

FAMILY PATTERNS: NUMBER OF
SUCCESSFUL INTRUSIONS

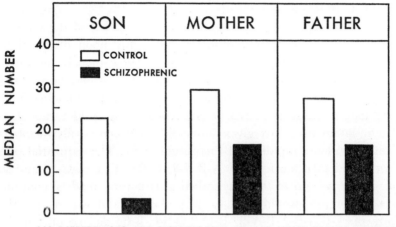

ALL DIFFERENCES ARE SIGNIFICANT AT .025 LEVEL (MANN-WHITNEY)

may be interrupted prematurely (before equilibrium has been re-established) or they may continue beyond their "natural" closure points. One would expect that well-functioning and efficient inter-action systems would be composed of alternating sequences of con-tinuous interaction approximating a theoretical optimal length, and that disturbed systems would be composed of excessively prolonged or prematurely terminated interactional sequences.

Verbal interaction that takes place in a dyad is called a *dialogue*. A dialogue consists of a continuous series of exchanges, or interactions, in which a statement by one participant, A, is fol-lowed by a statement from the other participant, B. The structure of a dialogue (which constitutes a continuous dyad) is fixed and allows for only one possible interactional sequence or structure: A-B-A-B. The sequential structure of verbal interaction in a three-person group (a triad) is considerably more complex. A *trialogue*, consisting of three participants, A, B, and C, allows for a variety of sequential patterns. Sequential patterns may shift from one to an-other, for longer or shorter continuous periods, with varying rates

of frequency from time to time. If, for example, two members of a
family remain locked into an interactional sequence and are impervious to the requirement of including the other, or of permitting
any shift in the dyadic structure of a trialogue, the family may not
be able to function competently.

One can construct four hypothetical models of the interactional structure of family trialogues depending upon distributions
of interactional sequences. In the first of these models the interactional sequences among the family members would be of brief
duration, no one member interacting with any other member for a
very long continuous period. There would be a rapid turnover of
dyadic interaction; any given interaction between family members
would terminate rapidly and then begin anew. The sequential pattern would take the form of A-B-A-B, C-B-C-B, C-A-C-A, and so
on. In the second of these hypothetical structural models, continuous interactions would tend to be prolonged and would take the
form of A-B-A-B-A-B-A-B, B-C-B-C-B-C-B-C, and so on. In the
third model, interactions between members of one family dyad (for
example, mother-son) would be prolonged and interaction with the
third member of the family triad would be either brief or absent.
In the fourth model, any one of the previous types of sequential
structures might prevail for a relatively brief period of time but the
interactional configurations would vary and change over time. Accordingly, one could distinguish between families that have rigid
and invariant interactional configurations and those that have fluid
and variable interactional patterns.

These models deserve further exploration to determine their
validity and to ascertain the effects that such family contexts might
have upon their members. That these patterns of interaction do in
fact occur among our own sample of families is illustrated below
for one schizophrenic family and one control family (see also Figures 3 and 4). These samples of interaction were taken from the
middle of each of the two transcripts merely for the purpose of
illustration. Each letter represents a statement by one of the participants in the family triad (father, mother, son). Spaces indicate
discontinuities in the interactional sequence.

Control Family

FM S MFMF S M F S FMFM SMSMSM FMFMFM S F MSMSM F FS
MFS MFMF S FMFMF SFSF MSMSM FSF MSM F MSMS MFMF SFSFS
MS FMFM SFS M SFS

"Schizophrenic" Family

MFM S MFMFMFM SMSMSMS FMFMFM S MFMFMFMFMFMFMFM
MSMSMSMSMSMSMSMSMSMSM FMFMFMFMFMFMFMFMFMF SMSM-
SM FMFMFMFMFMF SF MFMF S FMFMFMFMFMFMFMFMFM

It appears to us that the sample from the control family
illustrates the Type 1 model of brief interaction and that the "schizophrenic" family appears to be showing the Type 2 model of prolonged interaction or the Type 3 model with the son being the
excluded member of the triad. Our data show that excessively long
uninterrupted sequences of exchanges are more likely to occur in
our "schizophrenic" families than among our control families (see
Figure 14).

When we ascertained the length of the longest continuous
interaction sequence in each family, we found that the most prolonged interactions were found among the families with a schizophrenic member, and that these were most likely to occur as an
exchange between the mother and the patient-son. In fact, the
longest interaction sequence in four of the mother-son dyads consisted of more than fifty continuous interchanges.

We do not believe that our findings will come as a surprise
to clinicians who have frequently observed the occurrence of such
subsystems in "schizophrenic" families and have referred to them as
symbiotic relationships or as undifferentiated families. We have
already commented upon this pattern as a structural feature of
family interaction in our previous discussion of the distribution and
flow of communication to each of the family members occupying
different role statuses.

It appears to us now that one of the features of the interactional structure of a schizophrenogenic environment in disturbed

FIGURE 14

FAMILY PATTERNS: SEQUENCE LENGTH

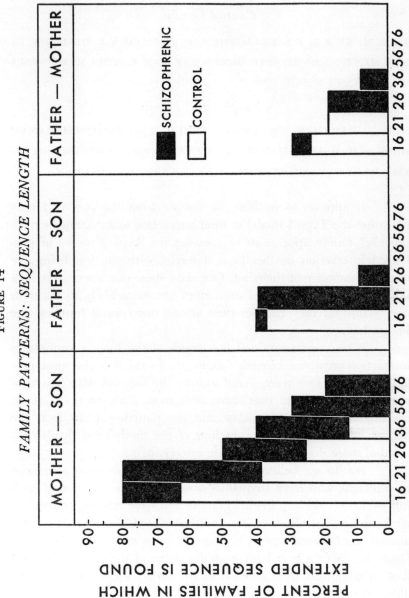

families is that the members operate in an interpersonal environment that does not facilitate a turnover and realignment of its component subsystems. The boundaries of the system seem to exhibit a quality of impermeability. When members of such families become involved in interaction with each other they seem to become "locked in" and are unable to disengage themselves or to be rescued by readjustments and realignments within the system.

At other times, such family subsystems cannot be established at all or stabilized because of unidirectional and nonreciprocal actions by other family members. Family interaction processes that exhibit such disturbances in their sequential configurations do not provide a context that makes possible the kind of collaboration among family members that is required for the fulfillment of the family functions of socialization and the successful execution of family objectives.

AGREEMENT, DISAGREEMENT, AND DISCONTINUITY

Identification and confirmation of self, as George Herbert Mead has noted, is one of the singularly important functions of human interaction. Through interaction, family members are affirmed as "human" and assigned statuses in social systems. Buber (1957) also writes that "A society may be termed human in the measure to which its members confirm one another (p. 101)." Among contemporary psychologists the phenomenon of confirmation or validation takes the form of the notions of reinforcement or reward. Among behavioral science students of interaction, such as Bales, the conceptualization is generally in terms of positive and negative reactions; more specifically, as agreement and disagreement in the stream of interaction. Bales (1953) tends "to assume that a preponderance of positive reactions over negative reactions is a condition of equilibrium or maintenance of the steady state of the system and also that negative reactions tend to inhibit the behavior which preceded (p. 124)." The distribution of positive and negative reactions, whether conceived of as a schedule of reinforcement, or as agreement/disagreement, confirmation/contradiction, congruence/incongruence, or support/attack, can be considered to be a significant characteristic of interaction in a social context, most especially in the family context.

A number of clinicians and students of the family have noted that lack of self-validation and frequent disagreement are distinguishing characteristics of "disturbed" families.

"One can listen to many hours of recordings of conversation between parents and a schizophrenic child without hearing one of them make a statement which is affirmed (Haley, 1959, p. 364)." "In those families of schizophrenics that have been studied in detail a consistent finding appears to be that there is minimal genuine confirmation of the parents by each other and of the child by each parent, separately or together . . . (Laing, 1962, p. 90)." In a description of the families of schizophrenic patients given in an early paper of Wynne *et al.* (1958), it is remarked that "it seemed clear that it was other than customary for the family members to acknowledge each other." Nevertheless, with the introduction of the concept of pseudomutuality, Wynne calls attention to the possibility that in families with schizophrenic members there may simultaneously occur "efforts to exclude from open recognition any evidences of noncomplementarity (p. 220)."

Since so frequent note has been taken of the confirmation/ nonconfirmation or accord/discord dimension of family behavior patterns, it seemed to us that it would be fruitful to develop some research methods for the study of these communicational configurations in families. The effort to reconceptualize and operationalize these communicational dimensions has been considerable, even though our effort was limited to the study of verbal behavior. For example, the content analysis of the interactions in the nineteen families presented here required more than six months of full-time work by two experienced coders.

Our decision was to classify all communications by family members in the study setting along an agreement-disagreement axis. In assessing communicational conflict and disharmony we were guided by the theoretical position of Bales (1950) and by some observations by Haley (1959). Bales suggests that all communications should be viewed in the context of ongoing sequences of interaction process; Haley views interaction sequences as involving successful or unsuccessful bids for control in interpersonal relationships. Our effort to quantify interactional agreement and disagreement is an attempt to incorporate both of these approaches. Our working assumption was that every communicational act could either explicitly or implicitly be regarded in some form as an agreement or a disagreement.

Explicit Agreement and Explicit Disagreement: The concept of explicit agreement and explicit disagreement derives largely from Bales' (1950) categories (3) and (10). However, to permit comparisons among the specific forms of disagreement that might be of special significance in comparing "disturbed" and control families, the category of explicit disagreement was further differentiated into five subcategories.* The data from these subcategories can easily be recombined to form the two major categories when required.

The clinical literature on families is replete with hypotheses regarding the *kind* of disagreement that prevails in "disturbed" families. In particular, there is the widely held view that indirect or tangential kinds of disagreements are more characteristic of disturbed families than are direct, outright attack and confrontation.

Five subcategories of explicit disagreement were developed for the purpose of investigating this problem. They were developed so that we would be in a better position to compare families in terms of their characteristic *types* of explicit disagreement. The definitions of these subcategories and a sample sequence of each are provided below. Only the first of the five subcategories concerns outright contradiction of the validity of a statement made by a previous speaker. The remaining four categories refer to more circuitous ways in which disagreements can be made manifest:

Category 1: Overt denial of validity of previous statement or contradiction of previous statement's content:

* Inter-rater agreement on the major categories was from 86 per cent to 95 per cent. Inter-rater agreement on the five subcategories (computed for categories with N's of 10 or more) was from 60 per cent to 80 per cent.

Example 1:

MOTHER: Remember that you promised that time that you would go to school.
SON: I did not. I never promised.

Category 2: Negative evaluation of previous statement's content or substance; disapproval:

Example 2:

SON: I wish their house would burn down.
MOTHER: That's not a nice thing to say.

Category 3: Qualification of content or substance of previous statement:

Example 3:

FATHER: They never did anything worthwhile.
MOTHER: Yes, I know, but you've got a short memory.

Category 4: Dismissal of previous statement's content or substance as unnecessary or irrelevant:

Example 4:

SON: Shouldn't it be fixed now?
MOTHER: This is no time to talk about household affairs.

Category 5: Sarcasm referring to content of previous statement:

Example 5:

MOTHER: I wonder if the doctor is married.
FATHER: You sure have a one-track mind.

Affirmation of the Self: Since one of the objectives of our investigation of interaction processes in families was to examine the effect of different interactional processes on the identification and affirmation of the self within the family context, special attention was directed to statements made by a family member that referred to his own attributes and characteristics of behavior or to those of another family member. All statements in which the speaker implied that "This is the kind of person 'I' am or 'he' is" were coded as *presentation-of-self* statements. For convenience, all other statements were coded as *content* statements. These two categories grew out of the distinction between "referential" and "expressive" communication originally made by Ogden and Richards (1938), and from Goffman's (1959) view of the interaction process as an exchange of "presentations of self." However, we conceived of presentation-of-self (or of other) statements as consisting only of those in which there is explicit verbal reference to the attributes, characteristics, or motives of persons. "Self" might be either ego or alter. In either case, the speaker is characterizing a person, either himself or someone else, or that person in relation to other people.

This category of statements relating to presentations of self was designed to make possible another quantitative approach to the amount of disharmony in a family. On the basis of clinical reports, we were inclined to believe that disagreements by other family members with presentation-of-self statements was likely to be a more sensitive indicator of family disharmony than disagreements with content statements—statements that do not touch upon matters pertaining to the individual's presentation and perceptions of characteristics of himself and of others. Explicit disagreements by other family members with presentation-of-self statements were coded into the same five subcategories of disagreement listed above for content statement. Some sample sequences are coded below for purposes of illustration:

Category 1: Overt denial of validity of preceding presentation-of-self statement:

Example 6:

MOTHER: You are the laziest kid I know.
SON: I am not lazy.

Category 2: Negative evaluation, disapproval, and so on, of presentation of self in preceding statement:

Example 7:

SON (*to Father*):   Why don't you have the guts to say you are not well?

Category 3: Qualification of preceding statement's presentation of self:

Example 8:

FATHER: I never did anything to the boy to hurt him.

MOTHER: Yes, I know, but that doesn't prove anything.

Category 4: Dismissal of previous statement's presentation of self as unnecessary or irrelevant:

Example 9:

SON: I feel very restless.
MOTHER: We've got something more important to talk about than your feelings.

Category 5: Sarcasm referring to preceding statement's presentation of self:

Example 10:

FATHER: Mike is really good at painting.
MOTHER: So good that I had to hire Bill to finish the job.

Each of these statements contains a contradiction, negative evaluation, qualification, dismissal, or sarcastic reaction to the presentation-of-self statement that precedes it. Each such response is treated as a form of explicit disagreement. It may sometimes seem difficult to distinguish a disagreement with a presentation-of-self statement from a disagreement with a content statement. For instance, let us consider Example 5 above, in which Mother says, "I wonder if the doctor is married." The statement can be construed as reflecting a personal motive on Mother's part (a romantic interest in the doctor), as indeed it is so construed by Father. But this is an inference not explicitly contained in her statement, which, taken at its face value, simply states, "I wonder if the doctor is married." The referent is (at least manifestly) to a question of fact: whether the doctor is married or not. Coders were instructed to make decisions about classification on the basis of this explicit level of meaning. For this reason Example 5 would be coded as an explicit disagreement with content. Now compare this example with Example 10, in which Father has specifically attributed to Son a capability that Mother explicitly negates with her sarcastic comment. Mother's statement in this instance is therefore classified as an explicit disagreement in the form of sarcasm) with a preceding presentation-of-self statement. It is also to be noted that the particular presentation of self with which Mother disagreed was Father's presentation of the self of the son. Our coders were also required to identify which "self" was being presented in a statement by locating each presentation-of-self statement within one of the following categories: (a) son's self; (b) mother's self; (c) father's self; (d) parent's dyadic self; or (e) self of some other not in the family.

Topical continuity and discontinuity: An interactional sequence exhibits the property of topical continuity when the statements in that sequence that immediately succeed each other are addressed to the same topic or theme. All interactional sequences that contain explicit agreements or explicit disagreements, by virtue of the fact that they revolve around the same topic, are topically continuous. Paradoxically enough, in order to disagree, interactors must agree on what to disagree about. In other words, every explicit disagreement is a form of implicit agreement as to *what* to talk about, and does not change the topical direction of the interactional sequence. Continuity may also be maintained by nonevaluative or "neutral" reactions. For example, consider the sequence, Ego: "What time is it?" Alter: "Half past three." In this sequence alter's reply supplies the item of information solicited by ego, and thus continues the direction and thematic focus of the interaction. Had alter responded with, "Do you have a match?" he would have ignored or terminated the thematic focus introduced in the preceding statement, and changed the topical development of the interaction sequence. This is the only category of response that introduces discontinuity into an interactional sequence.

Agreements, disagreements, and neutral (but relevant) responses maintain the continuity of interactional sequences. They all represent, by implication, agreements as to the content around which interaction is to revolve. We interpret only disregarding or changing a subject introduced by one of the participants in an interaction as an *implicit disagreement* on *what* to interact about. Even when interactors take opposing positions with regard to any substantive issue, they agree implicitly on the focus of their attention. According to Wynne and Singer (1965), families with a schizophrenic member appear to experience difficulty in agreeing on a focus. The parallel play noted in children and so-called autistic responses seen in schizophrenics clearly illustrate this type of communicational discontinuity.*

Table 2

TOPICAL CONTINUITY AND CLASSIFICATION OF AGREEMENT/DISAGREEMENT

Preceding Statement is about	Subsequent Statement is about	Evaluative Position	Classification
Topic A	Topic A	Positive	Explicit Agreement
Topic A	Topic A	Negative	Explicit Disagreement
Topic A	Topic A	Neutral	Implicit Agreement
Topic A	Topic B	——	Implicit Disagreement

PATTERNS OF AGREEMENT AND DISAGREEMENT

Does a quantitative study of interaction processes in "schizophrenic" families validate the portrait painted in some clinical reports of the presence in such families of continual and recurrent conflict? Or does it show that conflict in schizophrenic families tends to be indirect, and covert, as suggested by other investigators (Wynne, 1958; Ackerman, 1958)? This question embraces a number of interrelated issues: (1) Does the "schizophrenic" family context tend to generate conflict, as indicated by low concordance ra-

---

* In a pilot study, using sound films of interactional sequences, it was also possible to classify implicit agreement or disagreement with a topic in terms of nonverbal behavior. For example, implicit agreement with a topic introduced by ego could be shown by alter's moving forward in the chair, nodding, smiling, or making eye contact. On the other hand, alter's positioning his body away from ego, looking out of the window, tapping his foot, and so on, could be interpreted as implicit disagreement with *who* is talking and *what* was being talked about (Lennard, 1961).

tios (high levels of disagreement and low levels of agreement)? (2) Does explicit disagreement in the "schizophrenic" family context tend to be covert rather than overt, as indicated by the more frequent use of the indirect forms of disagreement (Categories 2, 3, and 5) rather than the direct forms of disagreement (Categories 1 and 4)? (3) Does the "schizophrenic" family context give rise to imbalances in the pattern of disagreements distributed among the three family statuses, as indicated by differences in the concordance ratios inhering in such statuses? (4) About what and about whom is conflict in "schizophrenic" family contexts centered, as indicated by the prevalence of disagreements with reference to content statements and presentation-of-self statements? (5) Does conflict in the "schizophrenic" family context take the form of implicit disagreement, as indicated by the prevalence of low topical continuity in such contexts?

Table 3 contains a summary of our comparative findings on the prevalence of agreements and disagreements in our "schizophrenic" and control families. This table contains a comparison of the mean percentage of agreements and disagreements and their ratios for "schizophrenic" and control families for both explicit and implicit statements, analyzed separately for content and presentation-of-self statements. Table 4 contains a comparison of the percentage of statements that fall into each of the five subcategories of disagreement.

Although many of the differences that can be noted are highly suggestive, none of the differences proved to be statistically significant at the .05 level. We nevertheless believe them to be sufficiently consistent and to be intriguing enough to be worthy of discussion and comment.

It is especially noteworthy that the differences in the frequency of occurrence of agreements and disagreements in "schizophrenic" and control families are not nearly so marked as one might have been led to expect from clinical theory and impression. Attenuation of these differences might be partially accounted for on the basis of the fact that discordance appears to be generally high in all family contexts, whether they are disturbed families or not.

The picture of the differences between "schizophrenic" and

Table 3

AGREEMENT AND DISAGREEMENT IN FAMILIES
(mean percentages)

	Explicit Agreement	*Explicit Disagreement*	*Ratio*
With Content:			
Control	11.8	10.9	1.05
Schizophrenic	8.6	13.8	.61
With Self:			
Control	1.5	2.5	.60
Schizophrenic	1.8	4.8	.38
	Implicit Agreement	*Implicit Disagreement*	*Ratio*
With Content:			
Control	56.7	11.0	5.16
Schizophrenic	51.1	10.6	4.84
With Self:			
Control	4.8	.6	7.70
Schizophrenic	6.7	1.8	3.72

control families sharpens somewhat, however, if one compares the concordance ratios in the two groups of families (percentage of agreement over percentage of disagreement). The ratios of concordance, in every category, are lower in the "schizophrenic" families than in the control families.

In the "schizophrenic" family systems, all concordance ratios are skewed more in the direction of discordance than those in the control families. Thus it appears that "schizophrenic" family systems do tend to manifest greater stress and imbalance along the agreement/disagreement axis than control families do, but the differences in levels of conflict are not so conspicuous as one might have expected.

When one studies the two groups of families with respect to

Table 4

DISAGREEMENT IN EACH CATEGORY
(mean percentages)

Type of Disagreement	Schizophrenic				Control			
	Son	Mother	Father	Family	Son	Mother	Father	Family
Direct:								
(1) Overt Denial	25	21	15	22	23	22	13	20
(4) Dismissal	2	3	5	4	5	5	7	5
Total Direct	27	24	20	26	28	27	20	25
Indirect:								
(2) Negative Evaluation	9	12	15	12	3	16	13	10
(3) Qualification	57	57	60	56	67	56	62	63
(5) Sarcasm	6	6	5	6	1	2	6	2
Total Indirect	72	75	80	74	71	74	81	75

the relative prevalence in them of the use of direct and indirect forms of disagreement for the families as a whole, no overall differences emerge at all. These data, therefore, do not support the suggestion that conflict in "schizophrenic" families tends to be more covert and indirect than in normal families.

Figure 15 displays the differences between the concordance ratios for each of the three family statuses and the family as a whole for our "schizophrenic" and control samples. The median ratio of concordance for the "schizophrenic" families is somewhat lower than for the control families, but again the difference is considerably less than one might have expected. However, a rather striking difference between the *patterns* in the two groups emerges if one examines the way in which the disagreement patterns are distributed among the family statuses.

While mothers and sons show lower rates of concordance in the "schizophrenic" families the fathers in the "schizophrenic" families show higher rates of concordance than those in the control families. The fathers in the control families show the lowest con-

FIGURE 15

FAMILY PATTERNS: AGREEMENT
AND DISAGREEMENT (EXPLICIT)

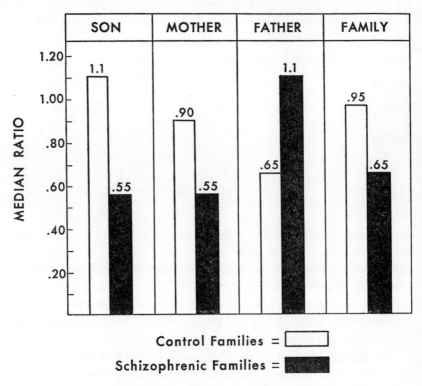

RATIO OF EXPLICIT AGREEMENTS TO EXPLICIT DISAGREEMENTS
FOR EACH FAMILY MEMBER

cordance ratio of the three family statuses in their families, while
the fathers in the "schizophrenic" families show the highest concordance ratios among the family statuses. This reversal in the concordance ratios in the father status may partially account for the
lowering of the difference in the concordance ratios of the families
as a whole.

Small group research has suggested that leadership involves
imposition of negative sanction and control. Hence one would have

expected that the enactment of an instrumental role such as father would result in a higher rate of disagreements. Finding a reversal in the agreement/disagreement ratio for the father in the "schizophrenic" family fits, almost too neatly, those theoretical formulations that claim that the father in such families has abdicated his instrumental role, and that there indeed occurs a role reversal between mother and father. Foremost among the advocates of this position are Lidz (1965) and his collaborators.

One of the reasons for which we undertook to differentiate presentation-of-self statements from content statements was our expectation that family discord was more likely to be expressed in the area of personal references than in pure content areas. Thus we believed that the frequency of disagreements about presentation-of-self statements might prove to be a more sensitive indicator of family discord than differences over content categories. Our findings in this regard are somewhat paradoxical. (See Table 3.) We found that only a small percentage of family disagreements actually revolved around this category in the particular context in which our data were collected, but still the concordance ratios for presentation-of-self statements did tend to be lower than the concordance ratios in the content categories.

A more intensive analysis of the data (from eight of the families) as to *whose* presentation-of-self statements were disagreed with *by whom* seemed to indicate that in schizophrenic families it is the child's presentation of self that is most frequently under attack—that is, his presentations are disconfirmed by the mother and her presentations (of him) are disconfirmed by him. This also appears to be true in the control families, but in the control families the mother's presentation of self also appears to be subject to disconfirmation as well.

The question now arises as to whether differences in the *qualitative* categories of disagreement will prove more revealing of differences between the two groups of families. Statements of disagreement, it should be obvious, will occur with a wide variation of intensity and affect. In some families, verbal expression of disagreement will be accompanied by great heat and even by threatening gestures; in others with warmth and sympathy. Many more qualitative differences in communication can be conceived of than can be measured, but in a study like ours, which limits itself to studying the transcripts of verbal behavior, qualitative differences can be approached only insofar as they are derivable from the transcripts of verbal behavior. If, for example, it has been claimed that in "schizophrenic" families expression of disagreement tends to be indirect, tangential, or oblique, then one must suppose these phenomena will be expressed in some characteristic of verbal behavior. Our division of disagreements into five subcategories grew out of a desire to test this hypothesis.

The overall impression conveyed by Table 4, which summarizes types of disagreement contributed by each family member and by the families as a whole, is how little "schizophrenic" and control families seem to differ in the relative prevalence of given types of disagreement. When we compare direct, explicit disagreements (categories 1 and 4) with indirect expressions of disagreement (categories 2, 3, and 5) we observe little difference in the overall prevalence of the use of direct and indirect forms of disagreement.

Our attention, however, was attracted to the differences in the employment of categories 4 and 5 in the "schizophrenic" and control families (especially on the part of mother and son). Both mothers and sons in the "schizophrenic" families resort to the use of sarcasm relatively more frequently than their counterparts in the control families do, though the total employment of this kind of communication is low in both groups of families. At the same time members in the control families do more often indicate to each other, directly and openly, that the topic introduced by another family member is not relevant and should not be pursued. Such direct guidance of interaction process does fit the conception of a normal better than that of a disturbed family.

This observation reminds us that differences among families (and for that matter all social contexts) may not be restricted to the content of the communications in that family, but may equally well reside in the characteristics of the interaction process of which the system is composed. Also it may well be, as we have argued, that differences in process (in the organization of the interaction process over time) may turn out to be as significant for understanding the behavior of individuals in different social contexts as have those approaches in which the content has been the main focus of attention.

The category we have called implicit disagreement or discontinuity is also a reference to an attribute of the interaction process—that is, whether a communication does or does not continue the topic of the preceding statement (or speaker). Here again we are dealing with a contentless, relational parameter of the interaction process. We have suggested that the introduction of such discontinuities into an interactional sequence implies a disagreement with *what* is to be talked about or *who* should be talking. From this point of view, every explicit agreement not only affirms the content of the proposition introduced by the previous speaker but also implicitly expresses agreement with *what* is to be talked about and by *whom*.

In order to assess the relative weight of explicit agreement over implicit disagreement in family contexts and to get a picture of the part this relation might play in differentiating types of family contexts, the ratio of explicit agreements over implicit disagreements was computed for each family and a bar graph was constructed in which the ratios were ranked in ascending order. These data are shown graphically in Figure 16 so that the reader can get an impression of where the schizophrenic and control families are located in the distribution determined by this index. While data from such a small sample of families cannot convey an unequivocal picture, the graph does suggest a possible trend on the part of control families to be located predominantly in the area in which the higher ratios occur, while the "schizophrenic" families seem to cluster around the lower ratios.

In connection with the above discussion we shall recapitulate other comparisons between "schizophrenic" and control families that have been presented elsewhere in the book. These deal, by and large, with formal process attributes of family interaction and reflect more distinct differences between the two groups of families than is shown by the analysis of the agreement-disagreement data. For example, we have reported and discussed that in "schizo-

FIGURE 16

FAMILY PATTERNS: AGREEMENT AND DISAGREEMENT (EXPLICIT AND IMPLICIT).

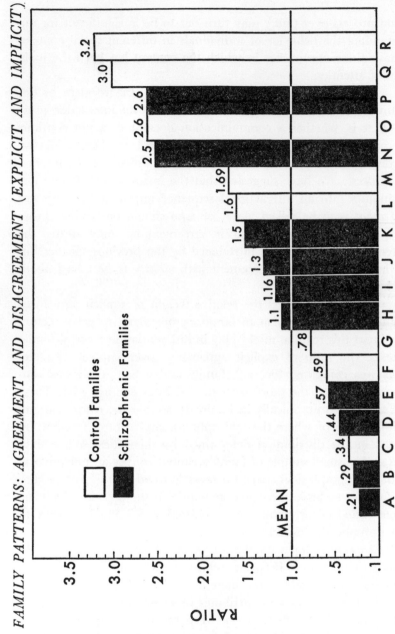

RATIO OF EXPLICIT AGREEMENT TO IMPLICIT DISAGREEMENT FOR EACH FAMILY

phrenic" families there occurs considerably less verbal interaction between father and mother and father and son than in the comparable control families; that there is less likelihood for any one family member to achieve entry into an ongoing interaction between two other family members, and that if they succeed in doing so, they are unable to redirect the focus of interaction. Moreover, there appears to be a bimodal distribution of interactional duration in "schizophrenic" families. Family members either alternate initiations rapidly without eliciting a response from the other family members or engage in protracted interactions without interruption. In control families interaction chains of moderate duration are found more frequently.

The analysis reported here and the findings reported elsewhere lead us now to suggest that the clinician's impression of differences between schizophrenic and control families in terms of disagreement and conflict may be derived from his observation of interaction process characteristics. However, such process or configurational differences are not easily conceptualized and grasped. Consequently, impressions of differences among families have tended to be formulated by them in terms of differences in explicit communication content.

PROCESS OF SOCIALIZATION IN FAMILY INTERACTION

Interaction involves unceasing interpretation and evaluation by each participant. The monitoring and labeling of intentions, of motives and of feelings enable participants in social interaction to engage in appropriate interpersonal behavior. Monitoring processes ordinarily occur "within" individuals and are not communicated. Indeed, it may often be dysfunctional for the flow of interaction to express them.

Accurate identification and interpretation of inner states followed by appropriate forms of action are essential for the care of an infant or a young child. During the first years of life, the mother and, to a lesser extent, the father, are required, at first, through appropriate tension reduction actions, and then later through verbal communications and representations, to identify, interpret, and respond to the inner states and experiences of their child. Bruch (1962a) stresses the fact that accurate identification and appropriate response to communications emitted by infants is critical for "the development of self-awareness—self-effectiveness (p. 20)." Lack of reinforcement, improper identification of or inappropriate responses to a child's experiential states can be expected to cause perplexity. The child then subsequently finds it difficult to differentiate among bodily states and may mislabel them.

> When a mother learns to offer food in response to signals indicating nutritional needs, the infant will develop the engram of "hunger" as a sensation distinct from other tension or needs. However, if the mother's reaction is continuously inappropriate, be it neglectful, oversolicitous, inhibiting, or indiscriminately permissive, the outcome for the child will be perplexing confusion in his biological clues and later in his perceptions and conceptualizations. When he is older he will not be able to recognize whether he is hungry or satiated, or suffering from some other discomfort . . . (Bruch, 1962b, p. 10).

As a child develops and matures he is expected to gradually assume this monitoring function for himself and the amount of labeling communication issuing from the parent diminishes. Such information as "You are angry," "You feel sad," supplied by a mother is then no longer necessary or appropriate to identify the state of tension or discomfort in the child but may in fact be dysfunctional. What struck us as we read the transcripts of conversations between mothers and their schizophrenic patient-sons was the pervasiveness of this type of communication as the mother's center of interest.

Illustrations from our transcripts are provided below as typical of such types of conversation.

Example 1:

MOTHER: Did you get any other feelings besides, uh, what was it? Getting mad, or you couldn't stand it? Was that the sole feeling you had?

PATIENT: I don't . . . .

MOTHER: Or was it a feeling of maybe, uh, and jealousness, jealousy?

PATIENT: Yeah, I imagine that is partly, partly jealousness. I mean jealousy. Partly I'm sure, part of it is jealousy.

MOTHER: Yeah.

PATIENT: Yeah.

MOTHER: Did you recognize it a certain, uh, feeling against Pop?

Example 2:

MOTHER: What do you call it, er, er, ant . . . not antagonism, that's not the word. What is that other word? Um, still, there's a hostility underneath occasionally. . . .

PATIENT: Shakiness like, er. . . .

MOTHER: Maybe a little hostility towards me sometimes which crops up. Er . . .

PATIENT: Do you have to use hostility?

MOTHER: A little, er, bitterness, maybe . . .

PATIENT: Yeah, that's . . .

MOTHER: A little . . .

PATIENT: That's better, or, or. . . .

MOTHER: A little. . . .

PATIENT: I, I think bitterness. . . .

MOTHER: Bitterness?

PATIENT: Yeah, er, the bitterness is something which I create myself.

MOTHER: Yes.

PATIENT: And you, and, and, er, I know it.

These illustrations call to mind the concept of "engulfing and intrusive communication" described by Fleck *et al.* (1959) as follows:

> . . . engulfing communication bespeaks the failure of a parent to establish ego boundaries between himself and an offspring. There may be a veritable barrage of cues from parent to child to elicit responses vital to the parent's emotional needs of the moment without any perception of the child as a separate person with his own emotional life. . . .

Lidz and Fleck (1960) go on to say that the mother of a schizophrenic child has "a tendency to confuse the child's needs with her own needs projected on the child; failure to recognize ego boundaries between herself and the child (p. 334)." This observation corresponds to the views of Bowen (1960), who writes:

> We have used the term projection to refer to the most all-pervasive mechanism in the mother-child relationship. It has been used constantly by every mother in every aspect of her relationship with the patient . . . [He describes a patient who] had never been able to know how she felt. She has depended on her mother to tell her how she felt. When occasionally she had a feeling that was different from what the mother said, she discounted her own feeling and felt the way the mother said she felt (pp. 360, 362).

In reading through our family transcripts we became aware of what appeared to us to be an unwillingness or inability upon the part of the parents of patients to abandon their monitoring function and to discontinue the labeling (or mislabeling) of the patient's inner states, motives, feelings, and needs.

We shall refer to all communications that refer to an individual's inner states (interpretations and evaluations of feelings, experiences, and so on) as *Level II communications,* to distinguish them from what we shall call *Level I* communications, which consist of nonevaluative references to human action, to events, or to other factual matters. Some examples of the two types of communications have been extracted from the transcripts and are shown below:

Examples of Level I communications:

MOTHER: Your grandmother and your grandfather when they came to the United States, they knew nothing about English. They knew nothing about the history of the United States.

MOTHER: Yeah, but a scientist, they can find something which can alleviate the suffering of millions or thousands. Like with all these vaccines that they discover. They rid the world of the most, the scourges of mankind.

Examples of Level II communications:

MOTHER: You feel that you're very sensitive?

MOTHER: That's what you'd learned, and you weren't actually

afraid. The only thing that you were afraid of was that you were really hurt. Is that right?

MOTHER: You only want to be good when you have to get something, huh, kid?

MOTHER: Remember, you said your head was shaking so, you were getting terrible pains in back of your head. You haven't had those pains since you're here.

MOTHER: You won't get sick. Don't talk it into yourself.

MOTHER: I'm sure you don't hate everybody here.

MOTHER: Well, you mean maybe you feel a little lonely with Bob around because you can't actually play with him?

We attempted to classify all statements made by the mothers of our patients into Level I or Level II types of communication. We found the median percentage of Level II communications for the mothers of patients to be 21 per cent, while it was only 10 per cent in the control families. This means that the mothers of patients devote more than twice the proportion of their communications to Level II as compared to the control mothers. The difference between the structure of the communications issuing from the control mothers and the mothers of patients is even more striking if one determines whether the content of their Level II communications revolves about themselves or others; their own inner states and feelings, or those of their sons. The median proportion of Level II references to alter was about .90 for the mothers of patients, while it was less than .40 for the control mothers (p equals .06).

That these findings result from parental unwillingness or inability to desist from their "monitoring" function and their persistence in labeling (or mislabeling) is also supported by some of our previous findings derived from the analysis of recorded conversations between four patient-parent dyads. Table 5 shows the number of times each member of these four patient-parent pairs changed the frame of reference from Level I to Level II, and from Level II to Level I. It can be seen that the patients in each pair persist in changing the Level from II to I; while the parents consistently change the Level from I to II. This means that the parents

Table 5

FREQUENCY OF CHANGES IN LEVELS OF COMMUNICATION

Parent- Patient Pair	Number of Times Parent Changes from:		Number of Times Patient Changes from:	
	Level I to Level II	Level II to Level I	Level I to Level II	Level II to Level I
A	41	10	1	33
B	17	3	4	18
C	61	28	18	51
D	21	0	0	21

direct the conversation toward the discussion of the patients' inner states while the patients try to direct the conversation to other topics. For example, the following dialogue:

PATIENT: Did you bring my laundry?
MOTHER: How do you feel today?
PATIENT: Do you have my laundry?
MOTHER: You look sad.
PATIENT: I'm O.K.
MOTHER: Are you angry with me?
PATIENT: Yes.

One cannot rule out the possibility that excessive preoccupation with a patient's feelings and subjective states may be a reaction to the child's disturbance rather than, as we tend to assume, being antecedent to the onset of the schizophrenic disorder and therefore possibly implicated in its development. Longitudinal data on a large number of families would be required to provide a definitive answer to this question. Or possibly an analysis of a control group of families in which there was a child suffering from a serious disorder other than schizophrenia.

Nevertheless, our findings are highly suggestive and, at this time, we tend toward the assumption that the failure on the part of parents to relinquish control over a patient-child's inner processes is characteristic of a schizophrenogenic context and we believe that the kind of interpersonal environment created by excessive Level II communications (especially if they reflect projections and mislabelings) is contributory to the genesis of the schizophrenic disorder. Our findings, arrived at through our quantitative content-analytic approach, are strongly supported by and lend support to clinically derived formulations to the effect that the mother in schizophrenic families employs symbolic communication to exercise control over her patient-child through the quality and structure of her communications.

These findings prompt us to offer a few speculative comments about sequences in personality and system control processes. We assume that in "normal" development, parents—especially the mother—through a set of mechanisms not yet explicated make it possible for a child to learn to identify and evaluate his own feelings, experiences, and motives. In time, the child can correctly interpret his own experience and is able to reject inaccurate versions when others offer them. Accompanying this increased awareness of inner states and their appropriate symbolic representation is the ability to set adaptive interpersonal processes into motion when the relief of discomfort requires actions on the part of another person. Thus, the child himself replaces his parent as the "regulator" of system process when conditions of intrapersonal or interpersonal disequilibrium require it. If a parent fails to induct his child into this control function or the child fails to achieve it, the child may remain dependent on the parent (as he has been as an infant) for restoration of intrapersonal or interpersonal equilibria.

Both with regard to psychic monitoring and with reference to labeling communication especially there appear to be optimal modes and levels (amounts) in specific social relationship systems (like the family) and for different developmental phases of these systems. Investigating the vicissitudes of labeling communication is compatible with the "system" conception of familial interaction. The occurrence of labeling may be used as an indicator of the type of homeostatic and control mechanisms that are operating in parent-child relationships and the changes that such mechanisms undergo as the statuses of the members of the system change.

COMPARISON OF GERMAN AND
AMERICAN FAMILIES

Much sociological work is based upon the assumption that shared group membership in larger cultural or ethnic contexts endows social systems with a special character. When one speaks of the German family or the American family, layman and scientist alike take it for granted that a family's embeddedness in a national group and its possession of a cultural identity lead to a distinctive tradition and a set of values vital to differences in the socialization process that is likely to occur in such families. From our point of view this inevitably implies the expectation that one should find distinctive role-relationship patterns and patterns of interaction within such family systems, if indeed ethnic, educational, occupational, economic, or national group membership define different social contexts.

However, there are few studies available in which interaction process data have been collected on particular social systems in different national groups. The studies of Strodtbeck (1951) and his associates (comparing interaction patterns in American families of different ethnic status) are among the few addressing themselves to this issue.

The problems in making cross-national studies are, of course, manifold, and social science researchers may have been well advised to avoid such undertakings. For how is one to go about selecting comparable samples of families and observing them under comparable conditions, using comparable stimuli to generate familial interaction patterns?

Our studies of American families made us particularly eager for replication of our approach within another national setting. For a number of reasons a cross-cultural comparison between American and German families, each with a disturbed youngster, appeared to be especially strategic. For one thing, we felt that a number of the interactional parameters (communication barriers, low intrusion rate) that have been postulated as being associated with disturbed families, are reflected in the stereotype of the traditional authoritarian German family of years past. If such patterns were generally more characteristic of German families, so our argument went, then German "control" and "disturbed" families might exhibit less differences with respect to these patterns than our American families. We therefore set out to replicate our study by collecting data on a group of German families. But although we were able to collect data on German families in a roughly comparable setting and with similar stimuli, we could not, with the limited resources at our disposal, really match them in a number of other ways.

For example, only a few of the German children would qualify as "grossly disturbed" or schizophrenic, as our sample of American youngsters did. Such youngsters, if so identified in Germany, are more likely to be inpatients with an "organic diagnosis." The group of German families on whom we finally did obtain some data were characterized perhaps mainly by the fact that they contained children who came to the attention of school authorities by virtue of some educational or behavioral difficulty.

Interaction data were collected on fourteen such German families, whose cooperation was enlisted through child guidance or educational clinic facilities. Our purpose was simply to see whether context, when conceived in terms of the national or cultural attributes of a social system (such as a family), makes a significant difference in patterns of interaction.

We are only too well aware of the dangers of generalizing on the basis of data collected on eighteen families in New York and fourteen families in Cologne, Germany. But once the data were obtained, it was hard to resist the temptation to determine whether they confirmed the proposition that families in different cultural contexts differ in their interactional allocations and arrangements, especially since the German family has been the subject of time-honored ascriptions by novelists, historians, and sociologists.

Our data for the German families do not reveal any striking difference in the pattern of utilization of the family's six channels of communication. The pattern of utilization appears to be similar to the pattern in the American families, with the medians falling about midway between those of the American control and the "schizophrenic" families. However, quite striking and provocative

differences did emerge in the pattern of intrusion attempts that
seemed to characterize the German families (see Figure 17).

FIGURE 17
*PATTERNS IN GERMAN FAMILIES:
INTRUSION ATTEMPTS*

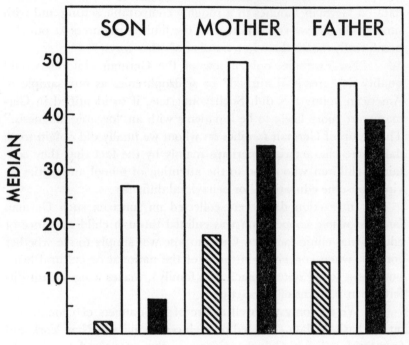

☒ = Cologne Pilot Study
☐ = U S A Control group
■ = U S A Schizophrenic group

With rspect to the median number of intrusion attempts,
every member of the German family triad ranked lower than members of American families. Members of the German families ranked
even lower than the members of the very "disturbed" American
families. To fully evaluate this finding, it must be borne in mind

that the absolute number of intrusion attempts that are possible
for any individual in any interacting triad is limited by the number
of opportunities to intrude that the others provide. Thus the person
who does the most talking will have proportionately less opportunity to intrude than will the member of the triad who engages in
the least number of ongoing interaction sequences.

To control for these factors, an intrusion index was computed that consisted of the percentage of times an individual attempts to intrude (intrusion opportunities divided by intrusion
attempts) upon ongoing interactions. The effect of this computation
upon the picture of interaction in the German families is quite revealing (see Figure 18), for it shows that although the fathers in
German families undertake intrusions less often than American fathers, they intrude proportionately more frequently. This finding is
explained by the fact that German fathers do most of the talking
in the family and hence have less opportunity to intrude, but they
nevertheless intervene proportionately more frequently. We also
noted that the German fathers tended to dominate and manage
family interaction during the research sessions, but we should remark
parenthetically that nevertheless the German families seemed to experience considerable difficulty in maintaining family interaction
even for the brief assigned intervals (three fifteen-minute intervals).

We have elsewhere observed that intrusion attempts represent efforts to redirect the flow of interaction and are indicators
of system fluidity and trends toward autonomy. In the case of the
German family, however, intrusion attempts may also reflect traditional role structures and expectations.

In a comprehensive review of studies of German national
character, Metraux (1953) writes that

> the central fact about German education (*Erziehung*) in the
> home is that . . . its focus is upon the training of the will.
> . . . it appears the young person . . . continuously has con-
> firmed that there is a necessary split between independence of
> mind and independence of action. . . . he learns that it is
> safe . . . to disagree with others in one's own mind but the
> expression of disagreement depends on one's relative position
> to those to whom one is talking.

Figure 18

PATTERNS IN GERMAN FAMILIES: INTRUSION ATTEMPTS OVER INTRUSION OPPORTUNITIES

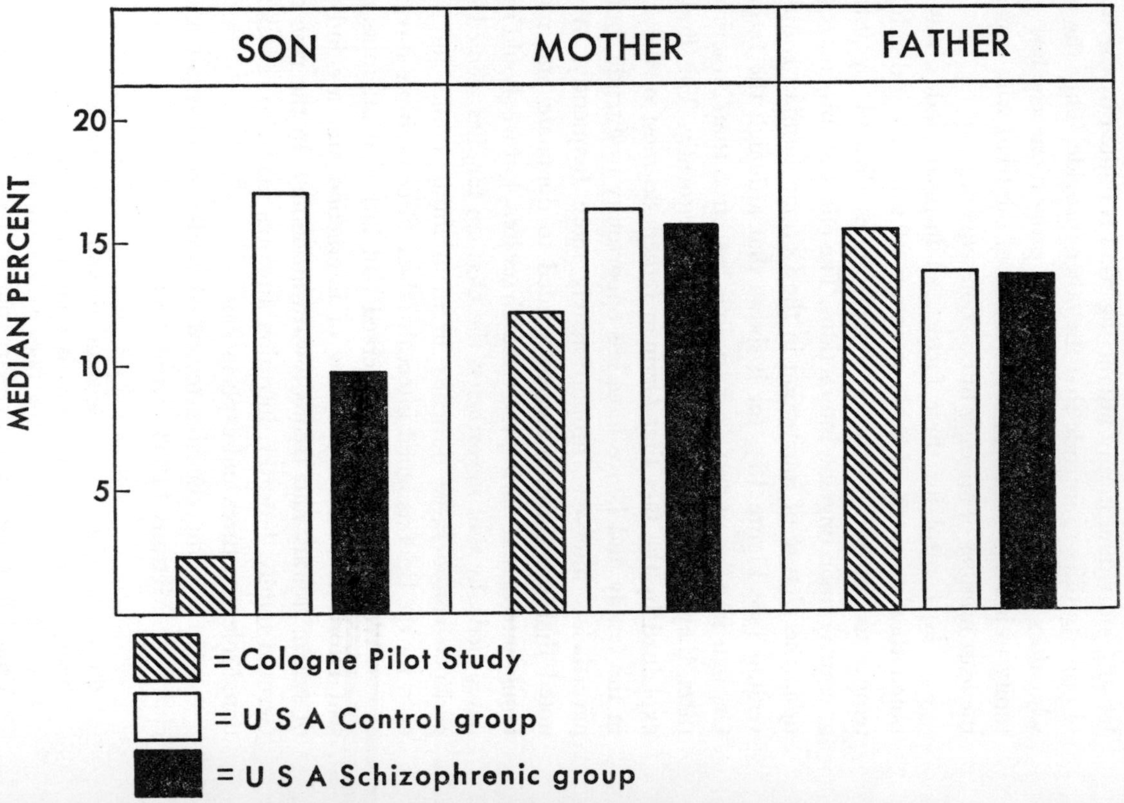
SON
MOTHER
FATHER
MEDIAN PERCENT
20
15
10
5
= Cologne Pilot Study
= U S A Control group
= U S A Schizophrenic group

These observations seem congruent enough with an "ideal type" conception of the German family of thirty years ago. In looking at our own tiny slice of family interaction process we wonder whether these observations are perhaps not so irrelevant today as some students of the German family (Mitscherlich, 1963) would have us believe. The roles of both mother and child in German family interaction seem to be more restricted than they are in American families. Redirection and control of communication processes is attempted by them only infrequently. The German youngster ranks much lower on this measure than American youngsters (even those identified as severely psychologically disturbed or psychotic). Altogether our meager data suggest a picture of an authoritarian family structure dominated by the father and one in which the child plays an almost passive interactional role.

In any case, our illustrative probe into the issue of the effects of cultural contexts on patterns of human interaction confirms our belief in the fruitfulness of pursuing this area—not only with reference to family systems, though these are of critical importance, but also with regard to the effects of national or cultural attributes upon transactions in therapeutic and educational systems and contexts.

Chapter 6

Psychotherapeutic Interaction

~~~~~~

If one asks a psychiatrist, a psychologist or a social worker what he does, he frequently replies, "I do psychotherapy." He appears to assume that whatever transpires during a therapy session is by definition "therapeutic." This attitude about psychotherapy is so much a part of the professional scene that it often obscures the fact that not only does *pathogenesis* sometimes occur within so-called therapy contexts but also that dramatic *therapeutic* changes occur within other kinds of human interaction settings as well.

Under the circumstances, it would seem relevant to ask what it is that so-called psychotherapy contexts share with other human interaction systems that makes them therapeutic or pathogenic, as

142

the case may be. Nevertheless, traditional explanations as to "what is therapeutic" about therapy have not been addressed to this issue at all, but rather have consisted of constructions of theoretical models designed specifically to guide psychotherapists in performances regarded as relatively unique to the psychotherapy situation and to the therapeutic role.

MODELS OF PSYCHOTHERAPY

Various explanations are favored by psychotherapists of different schools of theoretical thought as to why and how beneficial changes are brought about in a patient's feelings, perceptions, or behavior as a result of his interaction with a psychotherapist within a "therapeutic" context. Some of these explanations are presented briefly below for purposes of illustration.

Awareness of unconscious processes: Where id was, there shall be ego. Feelings, attitudes, and conflicts of which the patient can be made aware can be more easily changed or resolved.

Development of a regressive transference neurosis: The therapy situation replicates a childhood situation. Within it there is a reenactment of a previous childhood experience. Archaic feelings and attitudes toward parents are verbalized and examined. When maladaptive patterns of reaction toward parents fail with the therapist, new and more adaptive reaction patterns may emerge.

Cognitive information exchange: The therapist is an "expert" in living. He acts like a wise friend or counselor who has more experience and knowledge about the "ways of the world." He "decodes" the messages that are giving the patient difficulty. By identifying patterns in the behavior of the patient and those with whom he interacts, he helps the patient toward more effective solutions.

Emotional Release: The patient is encouraged to experience and express his feelings. The therapist invites and encourages the experiencing and communication of feelings, especially of feelings considered improper or dangerous by the patient.

Development of Social Control: If psychological illness is defined as "social deviance," treatment consequently may be considered a device for controlling "deviance." Control of deviance or "resocialization" is conceived of as the goal of therapy. Talcott Parsons (1951), who initially suggested the parallel between therapy and processes of social control, identified four phases involved in resocialization: permissiveness, support, denial or reciprocity, and manipulation of sanctions.

Behavior modification: Therapy is a reconditioning procedure. The therapist provides a schedule of operant reinforcement to reinforce or extinguish behavior patterns.

Enhancement of self: Through his consistent permissive and accepting attitude, a therapist allows the patient to accept and actualize his "self."

These represent only a few of many prescriptions and theoretical models that have gained a measure of acceptance among professionals engaged in the practice of psychotherapy. B. Nelson (1968) found estimates of as many as two hundred "techniques" being advocated or applied by American psychiatrists, psychoanalysts, and psychotherapists. As he says,

> Specification of the exact meaning and limits of the term "techniques" is a desideratum. Most authors . . . do not distinguish between rules defining the *mise en scene* of treatment (five hours a week, analyst seated behind the couch, etc.) and the notion of a strategic program or plan for which scientific rationale is available. . . . Very little as to the actualities of treatment can be inferred from the pronouncements of official representatives of psychoanalytic schools, institutes and groups. . . . Techniques are advocated by spokesmen for one set of reasons; they are applied by practitioners for another set of reasons (pp. 1–2)."

Exponents of each of these models postulate that the particular process described in their model accounts for "what is therapeutic" in psychotherapy. But little or no attention is devoted to an assessment of the role played in therapy by the interactional context within which all forms of treatment endeavor must perforce take place, and which they share in common with all social systems.

Nor do these theoretical models offer much in the way of constructs that are directly applicable to dynamics in therapeutic contexts other than the traditional one-to-one type of dyad—group therapy, family therapy, and the therapeutic community.

In the discussions to follow we shall explore some of the processes common to all therapy systems, irrespective of the particular theoretical orientation of the therapist. We wish to raise the question whether these more generic processes are merely correlates or prerequisites to therapy, to be taken for granted, so to speak, as simply providing a "ground" or context within which particular or significant therapeutic variables operate; or whether, indeed, these processes are in some measure essential and in themselves significant therapeutic components of any therapy system.

Paradoxically, many of the "system" characteristics of the therapy situation are precisely what the therapy situation has in common with other social situations, except that therapy brings people together for a rather unique purpose—to examine their own relationship. Perhaps this purpose is a major respect in which a therapy situation differs from other social situations such as education, work, and family situations.

Psychotherapy is a term used to identify a specialized social interaction situation. It is a term applied to any social context in which one person, designated as a professional, interacts with other persons, designated as patients or clients, for the purpose of changing them in some way regarded as being beneficial. All social interaction settings (especially those involving verbal interchanges) have features in common (rules of grammar, procedure, and so on). Like other interaction systems, the interaction process in therapy exhibits "system" properties such as interdependence, differentiation, and tendencies toward equilibrium.

Thus it may be that it is mainly their therapeutic objective that differentiates therapy systems from other social systems. The substantive and content components with which therapists tend to be preoccupied may merely provide the materials out of which a therapeutic experience is fashioned. Indeed there may be operative in any therapy situation an active therapeutic principle that is independent of the contents of which it is composed.

ROLE INDUCTION IN PSYCHOTHERAPY

Orderly social process requires some complementarity of behavior and expectations. Social systems operate without difficulty only if the individuals participating know their respective statuses. Obviously, different roles involve different sets of expectations with regard to both the self and the other.

In general, orderly social process demands the establishment of and conformity to a consensus as to: (1) who is to do what, when, and how often; (2) what behaviors follow each other (sequence schedules); (3) what attitudes and views participants are to maintain toward each other and to the situation. We will refer to role information of this kind (what a situation is like, what the rights, obligations, and expected behavior of the participants are to be) as *primary role system information.*

In most social situations, one of the participants knows more than the other about what behavior and attitudes are appropriate. He knows more about the rules of the game, the structure of the situation. He has a more specific or intricate cognitive map of the situation. For example, teachers, parents, physicians, psychiatrists, and employers are more sophisticated about their statuses than are students, children, patients, and employees. In fact, role-teaching itself is very much the function of many statuses in society.

The induction of children, new employees, patients, and students to the rules takes place willy-nilly, consciously or unconsciously, in daily social encounters everywhere. From this point of view, every social encounter can be seen as a potiential learning experience and each participant as simultaneously a teacher and student in a continuously reciprocating interactional developmental process. A parent learns from a child and a child learns from a parent. A psychotherapist learns about a patient and a patient learns about a psychotherapist. Needless to say, some people are better "teachers" than others, and some students are better "learners" than others.

Our concern here is to study communication about role behavior and the learning of role expectations that occur in therapist-patient systems. This view follows from sociological theory and research, which see the learning of appropriate role expectations as a prerequisite to the orderly interaction of individuals in different status positions.

The two persons involved in a psychotherapeutic encounter occupy different statuses: therapist and patient. It may be generally assumed that psychotherapists share many beliefs in common about their role, although their different training and experience may lead them to enact the therapist-patient role differently. Patients (or better, persons seeking to become patients), however, are likely to approach the therapy encounter with more widely differing sets of expectations. They often hold unrealistic notions about what is to take place during therapy. This may be due to a variety of reasons such as lack of previous experience or knowledge, or misconceptions derived from misinformation. Teaching a person who comes for treatment, how to be a patient and what to expect from a therapist is a necessary part of what must transpire during psychotherapy.

These considerations, which we refer to as attributes of the primary role system, transcend the details of the patient's special and unique personal problems, inasmuch as they provide the basis for every therapeutic relationship. Therapists frequently overlook this aspect of the therapeutic encounter and take it for granted, believing it to consist simply of practical details that must be settled before getting down to the "real" work of treatment. Consequently, there has been very little research on *how* roles (appropriate behaviors and expectations) are taught and learned during psychotherapy and *what* it is about them that is taught and learned. In our work we have considered three ways in which role-learning occurs during the psychotherapy interaction. For each of these we will now consider how the psychotherapy context serves to provide information and what is learned. Further, we will consider what interactional and system characteristics are relevant to the issue of role induction and whether the type of patient (diagnostic classification) makes a difference in the patterning of role communication in psychotherapy.

An examination of tape-recorded protocols of psychotherapy reveals that explicit discussion of the primary role system occu-
pies a considerable part of the early sessions of treatment, and, incidentally, role discussion continues to disturb the orderly sequence
of development of the therapy process if the psychotherapist does
not address himself sufficiently to the task of role induction. The
following typical illustrations of explicit primary role system communications (verbalizations referring to therapist and patient treatment roles, that is, references to the requirements, obligations,
rights, and duties of the therapist and patient; and the goals, purposes, and accomplishments of treatment) are taken verbatim from
some treatment sessions:

Therapist primary role system communications:

"Everything is relevant."

"Now here you are not criticizing, you are giving your opinion, your feeling, and it remains right here."

"Now here is a lovely opportunity for you to allow yourself to
feel so at ease, where there's no criticism. There's no censor,
there's no editor, you can really be yourself."

"I'm a doctor and interested in seeing how you feel now in
comparison to the past and what things should be done to
make you feel completely better, if possible."

"My purpose, of course, is to try and understand you in the
short time if I can and do anything I think might be of help
to you that I can do, by just talking to you."

Patient primary role system communications:

"What am I supposed to do here?"

"What shall I talk about?"

"Are we getting anywhere?"

"Can I sit up?"

In a previous study (Lennard and Bernstein, 1960), we
analyzed the frequency of occurrence of primary role system communications during the first fifty sessions of psychotherapy for eight
cases. The patients were considered by their therapists to be typical

psychoneurotic patients seen in office practice. We found that about 20 per cent of all therapist communications and about 15 per cent of patient communications during the first three sessions of treatment were classifiable as primary role system communications. During the course of treatment, we found a consistent downward trend in the percentage of communication devoted to this issue; so that by approximately the fourth month of treatment, less than 8 per cent of all the communication was about the primary role system.

A decrease in explicit discussion about the primary role system may reflect a decreasing necessity on the part of a therapist to educate his patient about therapy as well as an increasing sophistication on the part of a patient as to the behavior and attitudes required of him during treatment. Moreover, this teaching and learning of role expectations is not equally distributed within each session (Figure 19). Apparently sessions characteristically open with some exchange of primary role system information before a patient settles down to discussing his personal problems. Some resolution of the problems centering around the allocation of behavior in the treatment situation appears to be required in each session before the patient's personal problem can be tackled.

It is also of interest to ask what purposes explicit primary role system communication serves and what conditions in the treatment situation tend to generate it. It must be remembered that references to the primary system on the part of the therapist consist of instructions and clarifications as to what therapy is about; while on the part of the patient such references are requests for information about what is expected of him in the therapeutic relationship. The more primary system references there are on the part of the therapist, the more the therapist is affecting to teach his patient the proper role in treatment. Primary role system references tend to increase consensus and complementarity of expectations.

Dissimilarity or lack of complementarity in patient and therapist expectations would be expected to require that the therapist increase his efforts to correct a patient's inappropriate expectations and simultaneously to increase the patient's efforts to learn about what is expected of him. It was therefore hypothesized that dissimilarities in patient-therapist expectation would increase the frequency of primary role system communications. This indeed turned out to be the case.

Each of eight patient-therapist pairs was rated on a ten-point index of dissimilarity of expectations. The index was based on five parts of a question asked of both the patient and the therapist independently (Lennard and Bernstein, 1960), zero indicating complete similarity and ten the highest possible dissimilarity.

Table 6

THERAPIST OUTPUT OF PRIMARY ROLE SYSTEM PROPOSITIONS

		Index of dissimilarity (ranging from 0–10 High = Dissimilar)	Proportion of therapist primary system references
Therapist A	Patient 1	0	.09
	Patient 2	2	.27
Therapist B	Patient 1	1	.16
	Patient 2	3	.49
Therapist C	Patient 1	2	.05
	Patient 2	3	.20
Therapist D	Patient 1	3	.15
	Patient 2	4	.19

Table 6 shows the relationship between dissimilarity in therapist-patient expectations and the frequency of primary role system references. It can be seen in every case, if the two patients of each therapist are compared, that the proportion of primary role system references is always greater with the patient with whom there is the greatest dissimilarity in expectation.

Some therapists are more active than others with regard to role-teaching; they are also more verbally active in general than those who tend to avoid discussions of this kind (Lennard and Bernstein, 1960). Active role-teaching, it is assumed, results in patients' learning what their therapists expect of them in the treatment

FIGURE 19

*PATTERN OF PRIMARY ROLE SYSTEM
COMMUNICATION WITHIN A THERAPY SESSION*

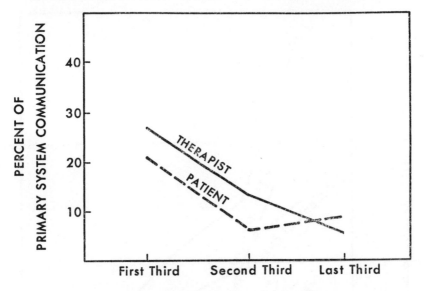

PHASE OF SESSION
BASED ON 21 SESSIONS

situation. But a comparison of the results of active role-teaching by
therapists upon the socialization of patients is rather strikingly illustrated by the data reported in Figure 20. There are three important
contrasts to be noted in Figure 20. First, the active therapists allot
many more propositions during the opening sessions of treatment to
discussion of therapist-patient roles than the passive therapists. Second, while the active therapists produce *more* primary role system
propositions than do their patients, the passive therapists produce
fewer primary role system propositions than do their patients. This
appears to mean that the active therapists take the lead in discussing the therapist-patient role, while the passive therapists seem to
avoid role discussion even when their patients introduce it. Third,
we see that in the dyads of the more active therapists, the amount
of role-teaching is initially large but diminishes rapidly, becoming

FIGURE 20

ROLE-LEARNING IN THERAPY:
EFFECT OF THERAPIST ACTIVITY

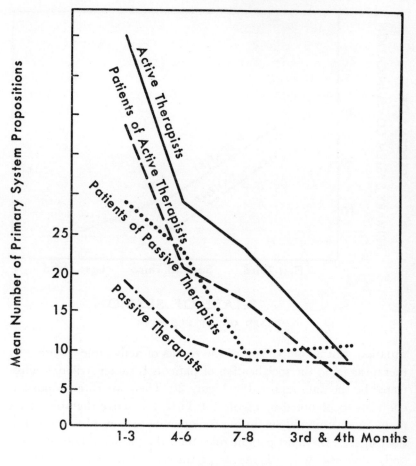

SESSIONS

OUTPUT OF PRIMARY ROLE SYSTEM PROPOSITIONS BY ACTIVE
AND PASSIVE THERAPISTS AND THEIR PATIENTS
(BASED ON 88 SESSIONS)

very low as therapy progresses, while with the passive therapists, the amount of role discussion levels off with the passage of time.

Of special interest are the curves illustrating the behavior of the patients. It can be seen that the amount of role discussion engaged in by the patients of the active therapists is initially much higher than the amount of role discussion engaged in by the patients of the passive therapists, but by the fourth month of treatment the situation is reversed. At that time, the patients of the passive therapists are engaged in about twice as much primary role system discussion as the patients of the active therapists.

Very disturbed individuals and those with poor prognoses, if they are "difficult to treat" or are "untreatable," may precisely be so *because they do not assume the patient role.* That is to say, they do not accept the conditions and limitations of the treatment relationship. They appear to suffer from a general inability to differentiate among role relationships and to behave in accordance with the specific expectations that varied social situations require.

Inspection of Figure 20 makes it hard to escape the conclusion that a considerable amount of teaching and learning about the primary system occurs during the first four months of treatment and that the greatest amount of orientation, reconciliation of expectations, and general "breaking in" occurs during the first eight sessions. To find any variable related to treatment that shows such consistent "movement" is in itself remarkable.

Let us turn now to some findings derived from our analysis of nineteen tape recordings of the first four sessions of therapy of five schizophrenic patients (three therapists) in the adult ward of Rockland State Mental Hospital and compare them with the findings of the first four sessions of our eight psychoneurotic office patients (see Figure 21). Seventeen per cent of all therapist communication and 14 per cent of all patient communication during the first four sessions of treatment of the eight psychoneurotic office patients (four therapists with two patients each) was devoted to discussion of the primary role system. But with respect to the hospitalized schizophrenic patients only 5 per cent of the therapists' verbal output refers to the primary role system, while only an insignificant proportion of the patients' propositions, .003 per cent, refers to it. In fact, in eleven sessions out of the fourteen transcribed and coded and reported in Table 7, the patients do not mention the primary role system at all.

Though Figure 21 reports data on only five schizophrenic patients, nineteen sessions are involved, and the findings are so consistent that one cannot help being impressed by the almost complete absence of primary role system communication on the part

Table 7

OUTPUT OF PRIMARY ROLE SYSTEM PROPOSITIONS
BY SCHIZOPHRENICS*

Patient	Session	Proportion of total verbal output							
		1	2	3	4	5	6	7	8
T-Z				.00	.00				
S-H		.00	.01	.00					.01
S-S		.00	.00	.00					
L-B		.00	.00		.00				
L-L		.00						.04	

* Table is incomplete.

Table 8

OUTPUT OF PRIMARY ROLE SYSTEM PROPOSITIONS BY
THERAPISTS WITH SCHIZOPHRENIC PATIENTS*

Therapist	Session	Proportion of total verbal output							
		1	2	3	4	5	6	7	8
T-Z				.00	.00				
S-H		.19	.11	.06					
S-S		.03	.00	.00					
L-B		.02	.00		.03				
L-L		.14						.07	

* Table is incomplete.

FIGURE 21

ROLE-LEARNING IN THERAPY:
EFFECT OF PSYCHOLOGICAL ATTRIBUTES

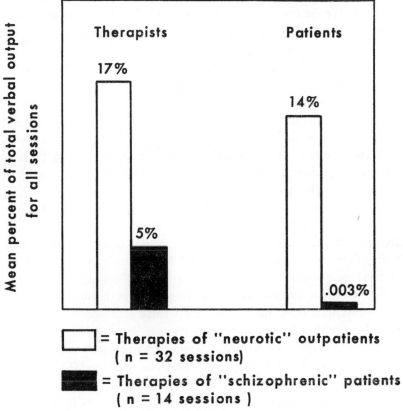

OUTPUT OF PRIMARY ROLE SYSTEM PROPOSITIONS IN THE
FIRST FOUR THERAPY SESSIONS OF NEUROTIC
AND SCHIZOPHRENIC PATIENTS

of the patients in these sessions. Even more impressive is that the
almost total lack of primary role system reference occurs in the first
four sessions of treatment, which are precisely those in which questions and problems about procedure and objectives are most likely
to occur. The hospitalized schizophrenics did not appear to have
engaged in any overt search for information or cues concerning the

structure or expectations of the relationship they were participating in. They did not manifestly concern themselves as to what behavior was appropriate and what behavior and expectations were inappropriate to the specific relationship that the doctor-patient role involves. We do not rule out the possibility that the patients were involved in other kinds of role-learning than that indicated by explicit role discussion (see the next two sections of this chapter).

This finding is a quantitative verification of what clinical investigators of schizophrenia have long maintained. Nevertheless, it would be unwise to lose sight of the possibility that we might be dealing with a clinical artifact generated by the long hospitalization of this group of patients (over a year), and their lack of concern with the structure of role relationships may be a result of hospital life and experience. More cases, in a variety of settings, will be required to settle this issue.

However, we feel that the magnitude of the difference in the frequency of primary role system communication between this group of hospitalized schizophrenics and the group of psychoneurotic office patients is too large and too clinically valid to be explained away entirely by the factor of hospitalization.

Of great interest, too, is the fact that the therapists engaging in psychotherapeutic interaction with these schizophrenic patients also show a very low yield of primary role system references (only 5 per cent) during the first four sessions of treatment, as compared with the therapists treating psychoneurotic patients. This finding means either that therapists who treat schizophrenics are different from those who treat psychoneurotics or that there is something about interacting with schizophrenic patients that tends to lower the therapist's output of role-teaching propositions. Our interpretation leans toward the latter explanation.

Further examination of Table 8 reveals that the therapists do attempt some role-teaching during the first interview with their schizophrenic patients. The amount of role-teaching they engage in varies from patient to patient, but is not distinctly less than the amount of role-teaching characteristic of the early therapeutic interactions of the four therapists dealing with psychoneurotics in office practice. But something about the experience of interacting with schizophrenics seems to discourage the therapists, or at any rate to lower the frequency of their references to the primary role system to zero within one or two treatment sessions.

Without in any way minimizing the importance of the traditional psychodynamic approaches to the understanding of the therapeutic process and without underestimating the value of personality theory in providing insight into the structure of so-called behavior disorders, we have focused attention on a different level of description, because we believe it is of great value and has not received the attention it deserves. Since psychotherapeutic interaction systems can be viewed as a special kind of social system, we assume that at least certain phenomena exhibited by such systems must be "system properties"; and that they should therefore be expected to exhibit, at least to some extent, the same lawfulness and order found in other social systems.

Since communication about role behavior is part of the larger total informational exchange system of which the psychotherapy system is composed, it should itself be influenced by certain of the general properties of information exchange systems. In our earlier studies (Lennard and Bernstein, 1960) we found some evidence in support of our hypothesis that the amount and kind of information fed into the system by the therapist was systematically related to the amount and kind of informational output by his patient and the system as a whole (see Figure 20). This viewpoint proposes that psychotherapy is composed of a very complex interrelation among psychological, structural, informational, and social system variables, and naturally thwarts any efforts to propose simplistic explanations of the psychotherapy process.

Absence of primary role system references on the part of certain people may be partly due to the discouragement of direct communication about the primary system in past social interaction systems (like the family) in which the individual has participated. Such an absence would reflect deficits in the socialization process. Schizophrenics, then, might be persons who had never been properly socialized to the necessity of differentiating roles. There is a growing body of evidence from a variety of sources in support of this conception.

Goldfarb *et al.* (1958) consider "parental perplexity" to be especially characteristic of the parents of schizophrenic children. He sees such parents as passive and uncertain. Bateson (1959) also holds that the parents of schizophrenics characteristically "strip" their communications to the identified patient "of all explicit meta-communicative material." He says that "from the point of view of the identified patient, there is, or appears to be, an absolute prohibition upon calling attention to the parent's incongruity in any overt way . . . (p. 133)." Inquiry about role relationships is thus interdicted. Confusion in parental role conceptions makes it impossible for such parents to induct their children into the appropriate reciprocal roles (Ackerman, 1962; Lidz, 1961; Wynne *et al.*, 1958). And Haley (1959) concludes that "The inability of the schizophrenic to relate to people . . . seems understandable if he was raised in a learning situation where whatever he did was disqualified (p. 367)." Under the circumstances, the absence of reference on the part of schizophrenics to the primary role system would be expected.

Systems of interpersonal communication seem to require some consensus, and some implementation of that consensus, as to the extent and rate of participation by each of the interacting participants. Moreover, for most interaction systems to move toward their objectives, minimum levels of specific kinds of communication seem to be required. Systems may vary with regard to amount of intrasystem input required, but most systems cannot continue to maintain themselves without certain minimum inputs (the participants fail to interact or the relationship dissolves). All members of the system need not contribute equally to these inputs, but it is probably characteristic of social systems that deficits in the contribution of some members of the system may have to be compensated for by other members.

Our data seem to suggest that social systems containing a schizophrenic member suffer from an initial deficit in the input of explicit primary role system information. If our view is correct that deficits in certain types of input on the part of one system member can be compensated for by another system member, it would seem that therapy systems involving a schizophrenic member place a special burden upon the role partner to engage in appropriate compensating activity; but evidently this is not ordinarily the case. The observation that certain interactions "go from bad to worse," seems to describe what so frequently happens in interactions with schizophrenic persons and their role partners. This unhappy course of events could as well be attributed to the failure on the part of the other system member to compensate for the deficits in input; and this failure may in turn prevent the system from achieving its goal.

The argument being presented here is in terms of social system deficits, not individual deficiencies. Ordinarily, failures of communication are attributed to the individual whose psychological functioning is impaired or deficient. We are suggesting, however, that in addition to such faulty individual functioning the failure of a basic system property (a deficit compensating mechanism) to emerge in systems involving a schizophrenic patient and a therapist may be crucial.

We have seen that in psychotherapy systems (with neurotic patients), mechanisms may be observed in which expectational and communicational discrepancies are reduced. For example, when independent measures (questionnaires and interviews with therapists and patients concomitant with therapy sessions) indicated a dissimilarity of expectations, we observed an increase in primary system communication.

There is considerable theoretical support for the idea that reduction of expectational discrepancies is one of the prime functional requirements of interaction systems (see Festinger, 1957; Homans, 1950; Newcomb, 1953). In situations in which there is uncertainty about the requirements of a role relationship, there is a tendency for participants to ferret out information regarding its structure and requirements. This is in part accomplished through verbal inquiries and definitions in the therapy situation, though no doubt there is also "motivated search"* for other than verbal cues that define the system of role expectations.

We would expect schizophrenic patients to have as little, or probably less, knowledge of the requirements of the patient role as do neurotic patients. Yet they make hardly any overt verbal effort to clarify discrepancies and inaccuracies in their perception of this role relationship, as can be seen from the virtual absence of patient communication about the primary system in the therapy relationship; yet therapists neglect to compensate by providing such inputs.

Therapeutic systems involving a schizophrenic patient, then, do not appear to exhibit the same tendencies toward reduction of expectational dissimilarities as do systems involving neurotic patients. Much comparative work remains to be done on the study of communication in "natural" or "normal" social systems, like friendship groups and families, to ascertain the generality of system variables such as those described above.

INFERENTIAL ROLE-LEARNING

We have already seen that psychotherapists devote a modest proportion of their communications explicitly to the task of role induction. Patients are told explicitly about appointment times, fees, and such things as the rule of free association and the confidentiality of therapeutic communications. But the major part of the explicit content of therapists' remarks ordinarily consists of other things, such as interpretation, reflection, clarification, inquiry, and summarization of the patients' communications. We believe, nevertheless, that role-teaching and role-learning occur concurrently.

Every action or remark by a therapist carries an implication beyond its content; the patient reacts to it on an inferential level. Every remark by a therapist carries with it, as it were, a meta-message. Like the therapist, the patient "wonders what he meant by that." Contents derive meanings from their contexts, and contexts can be defined by their contents. It is precisely because com-

---

* A term used by R. K. Merton in class lecture.

ments taken out of context lose meanings and because metamessages are lost that an interactional approach to psychotherapy protocols is so necessary.

Thus, in addition to what a patient learns from the explicit information he receives from his therapist, he also learns by inference. Fromm-Reichman (1959), in relating the following episode, provides a dramatic illustration of inferential learning:

> For a long time, because of her assaultiveness, a patient was kept in a wet pack during our interviews. One day she asked me to unpack her. After a short period of hesitation, I complied with her request. Later, when I reviewed the significant events which had occurred during her illness, I asked what she thought had contributed to her recovery. She responded with: "Don't you know that without asking? Of course, my recovery began the day you unpacked me. You were not too afraid to do so. That meant to me that I was not so bad that one had to be afraid of me when I was out of a pack. Therefore, your unpacking me made a dent in my discouragement. If I was no longer considered dangerous, I could get well (p. 217)."

Less dramatic incidents of inferential learning about the therapist-patient role occur throughout therapy. For example, what does a therapist imply to a patient if he asks for very intimate details of a patient's sex life? Many possible inferences may be drawn by the patient. Some patients respond with, "Oh, you analysts think everything is due to sex." Or, "Are you a Freudian?" A patient may infer that the therapist thinks it permissible to discuss tabooed subjects, or he may learn that in the psychotherapy context one discusses everything. Or he may infer that the therapist thinks that he has the right to ask anything. Or he may conclude that the therapist is being seductive.

When a therapist fails to respond judgmentally or to reprimand a patient who reports an instance of misbehavior that in other social contexts would merit criticism, the patient may be learning that within the therapy situation certain social norms have been suspended. Inferences can be drawn along a host of interactional parameters. Patients also draw inferences from what we might call *configurational metamessages,* responding to the frequency or sequence rather than to the content of a therapist's interventions. Note the conclusion that the young patient quoted below arrives at from the sequence of questions the therapist asks.

> THERAPIST: . . . Tell me a little bit about yourself.
> PATIENT: (Shrug) What do you want to know?
> THERAPIST: Anything you feel like telling me.
> PATIENT: (Long pause)
> THERAPIST: It's difficult to think of anything to start with? (An inference)
> PATIENT: Yes. (Long pause)
> THERAPIST: What kinds of things are you interested in?
> PATIENT: I like to roam around the University. I'm interested in math, chemistry, and physics.
> THERAPIST: You like to find out about things? (An inference)
> PATIENT: Yes. (Long pause)
> THERAPIST: What were you thinking about just then?
> PATIENT: I guess you are annoyed because I'm not giving you much information. (An inference) (Parker, 1962, p. 30).

One can learn by being *told,* but one can also learn by being *shown.* Being shown is a form of learning by experience. In addition to what a patient learns from the explicit instructions, explanations, and definitions that are provided for him by his therapist, he also learns much about the nature of psychotherapy by observing the behavior of the therapist. He may learn as much from what the therapist does as from what he says.

Much of the learning that takes place during social interaction is inferential in nature. A yawn may imply that it is time to say good night. A gift may signify love; a peremptory remark, dislike. An astute patient can learn a lot about what is required of him during treatment by inference from what a therapist says or does. Unfortunately, the distance between implication and inference can sometimes be very wide, and patients' conclusions are subject to revision. In the case of the young man quoted above, the therapist hastens to reassure him by providing explicit role-induction information. Therapist: "No, I'm not annoyed, although I would like to be able to find out how to help you if I can."

Role-learning in psychotherapy, as well as in other social systems, occurs along a variety of dimensions. One set of dimensions pertains to expectations about the *behavioral* roles of the participants.

Activeness: Who shall take the initiative in talking? How much of the job of verbalizing shall be done by each?

Ascendance: The status hierarchy; who exercises control and authority.

Selectivity: The relative saliency of topics to be discussed; what is relevant and what is irrelevant.

Reciprocity: The extent to which symmetry is expected to govern the participants' response patterns.

Concordance: The extent to which the participants are allowed to express their disagreements.

Formality: The extent to which the relation shall be formal as contrasted to casual; the extent to which prescribed semiritualistic behavioral patterns are to be observed.

A second set of dimensions pertains to *attitudes* rather than to behavior. Here we deal with dimensions that refer to how the participants view their behavior in a social situation.

Trust (Mistrust): To what extent can the interactors trust each other; especially, can a patient trust a therapist?

Hope (Despair): To what extent does the patient have reason to hope? Shall he abandon despair?

Freedom (Restraint): To what extent can feelings be discussed and expressed freely? Should discussion and expression be restrained? Should the participants maintain an attitude of caution toward their own and each other's contributions?

A third set of dimensions pertains to properties of the system or to the contract, rather than to the behavior or attitudes of the system members. These dimensions are expectations regarding the therapist-patient social system.

Goals: What will be accomplished by therapy?

Duration: How long will therapy take?

Confidentiality: Are the communications of the patient (and the therapist) confidential and privileged?

Constancy: How highly structured are certain arrangements (like duration of the session, appointment time, payment of fee)?

These dimensions of behavior, attitude, and the system can also be conceived of as norms.

All social behavior is governed by socially shared principles. However, though all social interaction involves a variety and hierarchy of norms, most such norms are implicit and remain outside the awareness of the participants. They may emerge into awareness only when their limits are transgressed (see section on Norms and Metanorms in Families). In fact, there is still somewhat of a mystery about the content or the variety of norms or rules that make orderly human interaction possible and about how these norms operate without their being to any significant extent consciously known by the social interactors.

Nevertheless, with regard to the dimensions specified above and perhaps many more, there prevail mutual understandings among members of social systems as to what is appropriate and permissible, and especially as to the manner in which occupants of different statuses should expect to relate to each other. For example, it is possible to elicit a description from any thoughtful person about any given context (such as employer-employee relationship) as to what level of intimacy and involvement was appropriate, how much criticism and discord should be expressed, and whether one or the other is in a position to initiate or terminate the interactive contact.

For many contexts there are also explicit norms that may be formally communicated through the issuance of instructions, guide-books, and the like. Whether such explicit norms "fit" the implicit norms actually prevailing in a given setting is an issue that only empirical research can settle.

However, the question that concerns us now is how the general norms governing all social interaction and the special norms that apply to the many subsystems in which persons interact relate to the norms that prevail in the psychotherapy interaction. In many respects these norms are bound to be similar. For example, we expect social interactional systems to share norms or rules regarding the recognition of a question, the discrimination between a statement made seriously and one made in jest, and of sequential rather than concurrent scheduling of verbalization on the part of the interacting persons.

Were it not for this similarity, any form of psychotherapy would become an impossible undertaking. The therapist would be in the position of a parent facing a newborn child and would first have to undertake the teaching of all of those fundamental rules of human interaction and language that are ordinarily taken for granted as given (and then, incidentally, frequently ignored) in the psychotherapy situation.*

However, the *content* of many of the norms referring to expectations and attitudes is different for the therapy context than for most other social contexts. In most conversations, for instance, it is inappropriate to interrupt, or at least it is improper to interrupt under some conditions; but in psychotherapy this rule of normal conversation is not in force. In most settings certain critical comments are permissible, although criticism is expected to remain within reasonable bounds; but in psychotherapy this norm is suspended. The conversational rule is that if you ask a question, you should expect some answer, or at least an acknowledgment of the question; but in psychotherapy one discovers that this rule does not necessarily hold.

The psychotherapy situation, then, is one in which many of the norms governing everyday social interaction are suspended or modified. We conceive of the "higher order" principles on the basis of which norms are transformed as metanorms (norms about norms). Such metanorms as applied in the therapy context, for example, affirm the special character and segregation of the therapy

---

* Parenthetically, it is for this reason that modification in the structure of psychotherapy is required in the treatment of young children, schizophrenics, and perhaps persons socialized in other cultural settings.

context from other social settings. The crucial principle that is in-
voked, often implicitly, requires the patient to suspend many of his
preconceptions as to what will transpire, what behavior would be
deemed appropriate, and how it is to be viewed. This suspension
of norms in the therapy context is justified, however, on the grounds
that it is temporary and restricted to the therapy setting, which
takes on an "as if" quality. Furthermore, in the therapy context
the expression of behavior and attitudes not ordinarily permitted
in other social contexts is encouraged for the specific purpose of
their examination and discussion and ultimately for the purpose of
modification. When either the message of the temporary or the
restricted character of revocation of norms is not clearly conveyed
or understood, the patient may experience considerable difficulty in
everyday social situations by what could be conceived as a form of
"acting out."

One of the by-products (and perhaps a *raison d'être*) of the
suspension and redefinition of norms in therapy is that, while this
suspension is being accomplished, norms governing everyday social
interaction undergo explication and examination. These very principles that govern normal social interaction, which, as noted earlier,
are ordinarily implicit, thus become subject to awareness. The possible "therapeutic" effect of such explication will be elaborated
later in our discussion of deutero-learning.

The psychotherapy relationship might well be described as a
metanormal relationship—a relationship about relationships. It is a
relationship to which metanorms always apply, and it is a relationship devoted solely to the modification, suspension, and redefinition
of the patient's norms. If a particular therapy relation is to be regarded as having been justified, such justification cannot be sought
in the metanormal interaction process within the system itself, but
can only be measured by the reflection of such processes as they
occur in social contexts outside of therapy. The "success" of therapy
naturally must be sought in improved interactional ability on the
part of a patient in education, work, family, and other social contexts.

CONTEXTUAL LEARNING IN PSYCHOTHERAPY

As a result of participating in a psychotherapeutic interaction system, a patient learns that in that particular social setting there are certain behaviors, attitudes, expectations, sequences, and programs that are appropriate and certain others that are not. His induction into the therapy system occurs through his receipt of explicit instructions and through inferences drawn from various therapist behaviors.

Such role-learning not only may represent a prerequisite for therapeutic interaction but may in itself be "therapeutic." This hypothesis will receive added support from the discussion of another mode of role-learning that occurs during psychotherapy (as indeed it does in all clinical settings). We refer to the effect of the psychotherapy *context itself* upon the patient. From this point of view, one may examine the properties of the psychotherapy context as if they constituted a kind of environment to which the patient is exposed and what possible consequences might follow from such an exposure.

That the attributes of an environment, whether physical, psychological, or social, can affect the behavior of persons exposed to them seems to be a truism. The color of walls, the temperature of rooms, the general mood of people at a party, beautiful and peaceful landscapes, isolation or a friendly atmosphere can hardly fail to have an impact upon people who are exposed to them. A statement by Jung (1928) quoted by McLuhan (1966) aptly illustrates this perspective with regard to a particular feature of the human environment.

Every Roman was surrounded by slaves. The slave and his psychology flooded ancient Italy, and every Roman became inwardly, and of course unwillingly, a slave. Because living constantly in the atmosphere of slaves, he became infected through the unconscious with their psychology. No one can shield himself from such influence (p. 35).

The analysis of how the characteristics of various social contexts influence present or former inhabitants of such contexts has
lately been of interest to social scientists (see Lazarsfeld and Barton,
1951).

The parameters of the psychotherapy context we regard as
significant for contextual learning are characteristics that more
properly fall under the rubric of process than of content. Being in
psychotherapy requires participation in an interaction process in
which behaviors are peculiarly allocated between individuals and
sequentially scheduled; which is periodically instituted at specified
times and for predetermined durations; and in which the focus and
direction of action revolve mainly around one member of the system. In other words, a psychotherapy context presents a highly
characteristic pattern or configuration of contextual parameters to
which a patient is repeatedly exposed and within which he must
interact. This contextual structure ultimately limits and shapes the
patient's behavior. Participation in such an interactional context
characteristically encourages a patient to deepen and accelerate his
further involvement. The successful experience of interacting in the
therapy context contains the metamessage: "You (the patient) are
competent and have the ability to function interactionally."

PROPERTIES OF INTERACTION IN THERAPY

We believe that the following contextual properties of therapeutic interaction processes are involved in the kind of role-learning
we have just described.

Duration: A patient is *assured* of participation in a social
context that can be expected to survive for a long period.

Noninterruption: In this context there is reasonable assur-
ance that the interaction will be scheduled for specified periods of
time without danger of interruption or premature termination of
the interaction session.

Total attention: The therapy relationship is asymmetrical.
Both the patient and the therapist attend to the patient behaviorally
and verbally.

Facilitation: Unlike most other contexts, in which there is
often a struggle between the participants as to who is going to talk

and about what, in the therapy context the patient is assured of almost complete freedom of expression without a counterforce being exerted by competition with the other participant. The therapist facilitates the flow and intended direction of the patient's action.

Continuity: Themes and topics are not deflected or disregarded but are likely to be pursued. The therapist endeavors to maintain continuity in content and mood between the patient and himself. In such an interactive configuration, the patient experiences himself as engaged in an interaction in which congruence and relevance are safeguarded by his coparticipant.

Programming: Many interactions do not go anywhere. Either one or the other of the participants does not know how to manage the development of the relationship or even a simple conversation. Patients may lack experience in taking part in interactions that appear to "get somewhere." To put this differently: patients may have had little exposure to sequentially "programmed" interactive contexts. The therapist, by virtue of having had experience in "role induction," is in a position to move together with the patient through the evolution of an interactive relationship.

Process analysis: In most social settings, it is dysfunctional to attend to the vicissitudes of the interaction process itself. In the therapy context, attention is frequently focused on the existential state of the interaction system. Time is devoted to the exploration of procedural and process difficulties that stand in the way of the development of complementarity between therapist and patient.

Differential threshold pattern: Patients are exposed to a context of communicational acts and expectations that places a minimum of strain upon their tolerance thresholds, so that they are not so frequently taxed beyond their ability to neutralize frustrating and discordant communication. Communicational balances are different, and the obstacles to interactional flow (*cf.* disagreement in family contexts) present in other settings are absent in the therapy context.

Boundaries: The therapy context is more highly structured and its components are more clearly defined than in most other social contexts. Temporal, spatial, physical, social, and intentional boundaries (frequency and length of visits, place, time, goals) are obvious and orderly. Ambiguity and lack of complementarity are thereby minimized. The patient has greater opportunity to experience "closure" in such a context.

These (and other) contextual properties of psychotherapy systems provide a patient with "contextual metamessages" and existential learning experiences. These contexts affect a patient independently of (although perhaps also simultaneously with) the particular contents of the interactions that occur within their framework. It is not our intention, in introducing this new perspective of the psychotherapy relationship, to replace the more traditional psychodynamically oriented approaches with a totally new theory of treatment, but rather to add another set of dimensions to those already formulated. It does not appear to us that consideration of the contextual properties of the system in which psychotherapy ordinarily occurs, nor attention to role-learning, contradicts in any significant way the more traditional ways of looking at psychotherapy, but rather that it places them within a broader frame of reference.

Nevertheless, this approach suggests some answers to some of the unasked questions and the hidden issues that have remained buried within the therapist-patient mystique. For instance, why do so many different approaches and techniques seem to have moderate success? What do various psychotherapy systems have in common with each other? What do psychotherapy systems share in common with other human interaction systems? Attention to the sociological frame of reference, formulation of new concepts and the definition of new variables generate a body of research hypotheses and a methodology for dealing with them, in an area sorely in need of objective research. Much work, of course, remains to be done. Data are available on the effect of one of the contextual parameters of therapist-patient interaction (that is, continuity), which will be introduced below for the purpose of illustrating this theoretical position.

If the metacommunicative aspects of interaction contexts do indeed exercise an influence on the participants, then *sequences* of communication and their *patterning* may be as important for the satisfaction of the participants and the achievement of the goals of the interaction system, as are the specific contents of their communications.

The hypothesis to be examined is that some types of sequences of communication are more "therapeutic" than others; that is to say, they are more likely to result in the participants' (therapists and patients) experiencing satisfaction with the interaction; in the accomplishment of the system's goals (as defined by the participants or others who have arranged for the interaction); and in changes in the behavioral patterns of the participants (the patients). Thus sequences of Type A should be more "therapeutic" than sequences of Type B, and accordingly a therapeutic system should exhibit more Type A sequences than Type B. Our hypothesis was that Type A sequences of communication would be likely to include the property we have identified as "continuity." Continuity refers to the relationship among the messages emitted by a single individual or the relationship of messages exchanged between individuals. A sequence of communications between a therapist and a patient is continuous if either the patient or the therapist responds to the other in terms of similar content (topical responsiveness), feeling, or category (descriptive, evaluative, or prescriptive). Let us consider the effect of topical continuity or responsiveness in interactional sequences on patient satisfaction with therapy sessions. Topical responsiveness is more readily identified than the feeling or communicational modes. It consists in the continuation by one participant of a topic introduced by the other.

In our previous study (1960) it was found that patients were less satisfied with sessions in which there was less topical continuity. Table 9 presents some new data on satisfaction with therapy sessions from hospitalized schizophrenic patients confirming this earlier finding. The longer two participants engage in discussion about one given topic or theme, the greater is the topical continuity of the interactional sequence. By continuing to talk about a topic introduced by a patient, a therapist contributes topical continuity to the interactional sequence. If they both engage in discussion about the same topic for a long sequence of interactions, topical continuity is high; if topic change occurs frequently, topical continuity is low. By counting the total number of topics introduced

Table 9

TOPICAL CONTINUITY AND PATIENT SATISFACTION
WITH SESSION*

	Index of Topical Continuity	Patient Rating[a]
Therapist A—		
Patient 1—Session 1	2.50	Dissatisfied
Patient 2—Session 1	2.64	Dissatisfied
Therapist B—		
Patient 1—Session 3	4.64	Satisfied
Session 4	4.86	Satisfied
Therapist C[b]—		
Patient 1—Session 2	4.50	Satisfied
Patient 2—Session 2	9.91	Satisfied
Therapist D—		
Patient 1—Session 1	2.08	Dissatisfied
—Session 2	2.52	Dissatisfied

* This table is based on data gathered at Rockland State Hospital. The data consist of transcripts of tape-recorded therapy sessions with hospitalized schizophrenic patients. The data are from an unselected sample of sessions that had been analyzed for "Continuity."

[a] From interviews with patients after each session.

[b] Patient 1 was "moderately" satisfied with Session 1, for which the index of topical continuity was 2.85.

into a session by a patient and comparing this number to the total number of times a therapist continues the same topic in his response, we were able to compute an index of topical continuity for each session. The index is computed by dividing the total number of therapist statements (in any given session) in which he continues to discuss a topic given in the previous patient statement, by the total number of different topics that the patient introduces. It can be seen that patients consistently expressed satisfaction (in a post-session interview) with sessions that rated high on therapist topical continuity (continuity index over 3.00) and dissatisfaction with sessions rated low on therapist topical continuity (continuity index below 3.00). Continuity in communication certainly reduces the amount of conflict and disagreement in a communicational system and probably also communicates a sense of being understood and of "being in communication" with the other, and of sharing a common frame of reference.

Chapter 7

Functions of
Human Interaction

~~~~~~

Human interaction provides the medium through which societies and, indeed, all social systems perform their functions and carry out their purposes. For, unless individuals interact, no social system can continue to exist. Nor can a society survive without an interchange of ideas, feelings, information, and other behavioral performances among its members. The simple observation that human beings must interact with each other appears to be so self-evident that it has been taken for granted by behavioral scientists and thus has escaped their more careful scrutiny and analysis. Consequently, some perhaps naive-appearing but nevertheless fundamental questions have not been asked. Such questions, which bear upon the *raison d'être* and func-

174

tion of human interaction do, however, deserve careful and searching consideration.

Interaction serves survival functions for both individuals and groups. Subsidiary purposes such as information exchange, socialization, and the maintenance of physical well-being are also accomplished through this means. These functions are important, for example, for the maintenance of family systems, which require interaction between parents and children for the purpose of socialization and for information exchange.

Different social contexts often demand different patterns of interaction among individuals within them for the maintenance of the social system. Studies of interaction patterns in different specific social contexts (such as the family context, work situations, psychotherapy, hospital contexts) show a dependency of interaction patterns upon the requirements of the social context. The pattern of interaction in a work situation is different from that within a family, which is, in turn, different from that to be found in psychotherapy.

Social systems or contexts evolve as a response to interrelated societal demands and requirements. The structural features of a system as well as the interactive arrangements that prevail within it represent particular *solutions* to the problems posed. Unfortunately, it not infrequently happens that the interaction patterns generated within a given social context are dysfunctional, either in relation to the accomplishment of the purposes for which the system was instituted or to the individual members of the system, or to both. The *raison d'être* of a particular social context may already presage the emergence of such dysfunctions. For example, once a military establishment has been created, it is quite likely that concern for an individual may have to be sacrificed for the sake of accomplishing military objectives.

Patterns and sequences of human interaction prevailing in some kinds of social contexts often result in unanticipated but nonetheless disastrous consequences for system members. We are thinking here of the interactional arrangements prevailing in such social contexts as traditional mental hospitals, prisons, and in socially disadvantaged or disturbed families. Interaction patterns should be

considered unsatisfactory or pathological if they are inimical either
to the well-being of the individual or to the full development and
survival of the social system which they comprise. In the event that
the behavioral requirements of a social system and those of the individuals within it lack complementarity, the emergent interactional
patterns will reflect this incompatibility.

One need not deny the possible role of biological or genetic
factors to share the view of *homo homini lupus*. Misery, unhappi-
ness, and developmental defects certainly derive from aberrations
in the patterning of social interaction. Nor need such "pathogenic"
sequences of interaction necessarily be ascribed to malevolence inhering in individuals or to "evils" of given social systems. The
"guilty" participants in a social process may sometimes be as much
"victims" of their own interactional experience, cognitive exposure,
and informational deprivation as those who are ordinarily seen as
their victims. The crux of our thesis lies precisely here. Very often
the context or system places constraints upon the latitude and effectiveness of efforts to relieve the plight of individuals caught in such
social contexts or situations. Not only do these "pathological" contexts thwart the individuals within them, but, more significantly
for the application of therapeutic, rehabilitative, and reparative
programs, these contexts thwart any efforts to intervene at the level
of the individual without changing the situation. Many well-meaning programs of education and psychotherapy have foundered in
ghettos, prisons, and mental institutions because of their failure to
take account of the systems in which they were undertaken. When
such is the case, we believe it necessary to try to identify the attributes of interactional sequences that are to be characterized as
pathogenic and those to be characterized as therapeutic, in order
to be able to offer suggestions as to what changes or interventions
at the system level might be indicated to render contexts less noxious
or more therapeutic.

Furthermore, one must be concerned with defining system
states and system properties that reflect inadequate system development and that portend a subsequent failure to achieve the goals
for which a particular system has been instituted or that foreshadow

the eventual disintegration of that system. Note that in our appraisal we shift back and forth from a focus on interactional sequences to a focus on social system properties. The reason for this shifting is that in our theoretical perspective, we conceive of system properties as made manifest in the form of interactional sequences and of interactional sequences as determined by system processes.

Although we do not yet know enough about the kinds of interaction that lead participants in an interaction system to become disabled, impaired, or unable to function, we do have a variety of sources to draw upon from which to assemble a number of hypotheses about what is pathogenic or damaging interaction—the kind of interaction one would not want to engage in with patients, in the role of therapist, with children, in the role of parent, or with students, in the role of teacher.

Our research and the interactional perspective give rise to a number of hypotheses as to what attributes would characterize such therapeutic or pathogenic interactional processes and social system properties.

The properties of interaction that we wish to identify as pathogenic are those that apply equally well to pathological interaction in a variety of different social contexts (from family to mental hospital), while those we shall characterize as therapeutic apply equally well to interaction patterns in a healthy family and interaction in a well-conducted psychotherapy experience.

In system property terms, the difference between a pathological attribute and a therapeutic attribute is often a quantitative difference. Thus, it is often not a question of whether a particular attribute is present or absent, but rather a question of frequencies, thresholds, equilibria, over-time variations, and relationships with other system variables. Accordingly, the discussion of what is pathological is often the other side of the coin of what is therapeutic. This notion will become clearer as our discussion proceeds, but perhaps an illustration will prove helpful: imperviousness to interaction, which is a pathogenic attribute in a social system, is a lack (or below threshold frequency) of responsiveness, which is a therapeutic attribute.

THERAPEUTIC INTERACTION

We have consistently stressed the view that an analysis of the arrangements of communicative behaviors in social systems is the most promising avenue for understanding the effects of social contexts. Certain attributes of interactive processes, when they are viewed as a context to which system members are exposed, can be conceived of as being either beneficial or harmful to the functioning and well-being of the members of such systems.

Social behavior can be viewed either as self-initiated (stimulated from within the individual) or as reactive (triggered or demanded from the outside); and as either autonomous (expressive of the individual's own feelings and experience) or dependent (controlled by others).

ENCOURAGEMENT OF SELF-INITIATED BEHAVIOR

Social contexts generate widely disparate distributions and balances among initiated and responsive acts. We believe that social systems in which some members overspecialize or are forced to specialize in one type of behavior only (for example, are forced to engage in responsive behavior only) are inimical both to the growth of the system and to the integrity of the individual members of the system.

In our studies of families with a schizophrenic child we found that such families tend to discourage forms of behavior (especially on the part of the child) for which the term *self-initiated* would be appropriate—for example, interactional intrusions. Intrusions represent attempts to modify the structure of participation and to redirect the focus of group attention. The number and successfulness of intrusions are indicators of the extent to which self-initiated behavior is tolerated by a group. The ignoring of intrusions tends to decrease the occurrence of unsolicited behavioral acts.

We concluded that the opportunity to experience success in expressing self-initiated behavior is excessively limited in schizophrenic family contexts; that, indeed, there is an imbalance in the communicational environment within such families that favors the reinforcement of "controlled or reactive" behavioral acts only.

We believe that interactional contexts can be considered therapeutic when options regarding *who* is to interact, *when,* and *about what,* are maximized; when the initiating of contact and the allocation of attention is optimally balanced among the participants. The willingness of a sensitive parent or a clinician to let a child or a patient initiate contacts and to define the focus of interaction testifies to an intuitive grasp of this phenomenon.

Pathogenic interaction contexts seem to be characterized by imperviousness to the transmission of, or modification by, stimuli or messages emitted by some members. Their messages or behaviors are not acknowledged, and the interactional potential of these participants in such contexts is thereby minimized. These systems members are likely to suffer the greatest strain. Hospitalized patients and family "scapegoats" are often the nexus of such contextual stress.

Our studies have indicated that in therapy systems, themes and topics introduced by patient members are likely to be acknowledged and pursued. In these interaction systems continuity of behaviors and messages (introduced by the "weaker" member, the one whose initiative, or autonomous potential, has been crippled) are preserved.

ENCOURAGEMENT OF AUTONOMOUS BEHAVIOR

Interaction contexts that restrain the introduction of self-initiated or unsolicited behaviors into the system also tend to disallow autonomy. Such contexts evidently provide sufficient opportunity neither for self-expression nor for self-formulations about the nature of personal experiences and feelings, especially for infants and children reared within them.

Clinical investigators like Laing (1965) and Bruch (1962a) have identified a process they call "mystification" or "falsification" as characteristically present in severely disturbed families. Both of these phenomena are accomplished by what we have already referred to as "labeling communication" (communications that interpret, evaluate, or label another person's inner states, motives, or experiences). Mystification or falsification, of course, results from *mislabeling*. In our own study of interaction in family contexts, we found a greater prevalence of labeling (mislabeling) communications present in disturbed family contexts than in control families.

It appears to us that an excess of labeling and mislabeling communication would be characteristic of social systems with disturbed equilibrating or repair mechanisms, and in this sense it is an indicator of a potentially pathogenic interaction context. Although we use the family context to illustrate the reciprocal relationship between homeostasis and system mechanisms and to illustrate the emergence of mislabeling or mystifying communications, our analysis can be applied to other pathogenic social contexts as well, such as are found in a traditional mental hospital setting or, even as Karl Marx would maintain, in a political setting.

We have already elaborated upon the therapeutic function of labeling in an earlier section (see Socialization Process in Family Interaction Systems) as the means by which an individual develops autonomy through internalizing the "monitoring" or parenting role. However, when labeling communication is persistently present or increases in frequency of use throughout the life of a social system, we assume this to reflect a failure in "normal" system development, and we consider it to be dysfunctional and damaging both to the system and to the individuals in that system.

Mislabeling or mystification, however, appears to us to be dysfunctional for the individual in almost every context. Because mislabeling is dysfunctional for a social system and its members, we regard it as a pathological means for maintaining homeostasis. In the following passage, Spiegel (1957) analyzes an example of what he calls "masking" in much the same way:

A child bumps himself on a chair, and the mother says, "Naughty chair!" . . . . Why does she do this? Pain produces anger and in order to avoid the potential role conflict which may be precipitated between herself and her child . . . she denies the potential negative evaluation of herself as insufficiently protective of the child, by displacing the carelessness to the chair. This preserves equilibrium between herself and the child and thus is functional for their role system. . . . But

. . . what is functional for their role system may . . . be dysfunctional for the child's ability to test reality. She conceals the important information that pain and accidents can occur without motive and need to be endured in the inevitable process of maturation and acquisition of autonomy by the child . . . (p. 12).

Like other social systems, family systems differ in their ability to cope with diversity and conflict; to cope with what we have called extrasystem and intrasystem inputs. For some families, the balance is so fragile, or their homeostatic potential is so limited, that the very existence of disparate dispositions, perceptions, or inner experiences among family members constitutes a source of unbearable system strain that threatens the survival of the family system or its members. Labeling interaction (mislabeling) in such family contexts often may then be called into play to forestall the introduction into the system of feelings, intentions or goals on the part of family members (especially, new members) that might require the employment of homeostatic mechanisms for the establishment of new levels of adaptation. In such families, differentiated roles or differentiated personalities are avoided at all costs in order to obviate the necessity for system readjustments due to the conflict and negotiation that differentiation generates and that normal family development requires. They thus use mislabeling to establish a pseudo-homeostasis—stability through nonadjustment rather than through readjustment.

Communications among members of a social system about one another's inner experiences and about intentions are employed within social systems both to achieve consensus and to establish or to maintain uniform and nonconflictual versions of feelings and behavior. Exchange of information reduces strain and expectational dissimilarity. However, when consensus is achieved through mislabeling and mystification, it causes a further and perhaps even more serious disequilibration in the intrapersonal systems of family members. Confronting an individual with mystifying versions of his experience that are incompatible with his biological and psychological requirements diminishes the individual's understanding and control of his own experiences and action.

ENHANCEMENT OF SOCIALIZATION AND LEARNING

Interaction contexts that provide high levels of information, definition of roles, and primary system information regarding appropriate and expected behaviors on the part of the participants may be viewed as therapeutic.

In most social situations, one participant knows more than the other about what behaviors and attitudes are appropriate. He knows about the rules and requirements of the context in which the interactors find themselves and within which they will have to continue to interact. Induction of children, patients, students, new employees, and other novices to both process and role requirements takes place continuously in family, therapy, educational, and occupational contexts. Every social encounter represents a potential learning experience. Participants are simultaneously teachers and students in a continuously reciprocating interactional developmental process.

Because successful participation in social situations requires complementarity of expectations and behavior, contexts may be regarded as pathogenic when the level of role and primary system information provided in the course of interaction falls below the level required for appropriate functioning of system members. Untoward outcomes for the system and its members may result when the type of role prescriptions and instructions are poorly conveyed and are ambiguous. In their studies of families with schizophrenic youngsters, Goldfarb (1958) and his associates were struck by the ambiguous and inadequate manner in which the children were socialized into sex- and age-appropriate behaviors in such families. In our own studies of psychotherapy systems, we found that, during the initial stages of psychotherapy interaction involving neurotic patients in office settings, a considerable amount of interaction was devoted to role instructions and clarification. However, we observed very little interaction revolving around role instructions in therapy systems involving schizophrenic patients in hospital settings. This deficit in primary role system communication was very notable, not only on the part of the patients from whom it might have been expected, but also on the part of the therapists.

In our view, a minimum amount of socialization is required in order to generate or to maintain any social system. A failure to provide such minimal levels of socialization information in the course of interaction is, in our view, responsible for the failure of many social systems (whether family or therapy) to achieve their goals.

Family and therapy systems, of course, have dual objectives. They must socialize their members to function within them, but they must also teach their members how to function in other social contexts. They accomplish both of these objectives successfully as long as the two tasks remain complementary. They fail when one objective conflicts with the other. Hence when a family context gives rise, for example, to mystification for system maintenance, not only does it fail to accomplish its own primary task of role induction, but it becomes a context ill-suited to perform its secondary goal of teaching its members how to behave properly in other social contexts. Moreover, as a result of their participation in such an idiosyncratic social context, which is itself functioning defectively, the necessary deutero-learning about social interaction and role-learning fails to occur, further impairing the individual's capacity to cope with other social situations.

Interaction process is a major means through which role induction is accomplished. When the pattern of interaction process is such that adequate levels of role information and instructions are not provided, an untoward effect often occurs both upon system members and upon the achievement of the system's goals. We hypothesize that such untoward effects might be reversed or at least allayed through either an increase in the level of socialization inputs within the system, or through transfer of the system members into other social systems (for example, therapy, foster family, therapeutic community) in which a higher level of direct and unequivocal role information prevails.

REDUCTION OF STRESS AND DISCORDANCE

Patterns of human interaction vary in both quantitative and qualitative characteristics and may, therefore, generate difficulties for individuals along either continuum. Certain qualitative contents of communication are easier to cope with than others, thus positive and supportive communications create less stress than negative and demeaning ones. But of equal importance in determining the difficulty an individual will have in interacting within a given social context is the *quantity* of such noxious communications and their distribution over time. Such difficulties may arise not only from *aggregates* of certain types of communication (such as hostile, demeaning, or deceptive behaviors) but also from the *quantitative imbalances* in the distributions of given kinds of communication that may characterize a pattern of interaction, as, for example, imbalances between positive and negative statements. Singer (1967), referring to a series of significant studies on communication patterns of schizophrenic patients, conducted with Lyman Wynne, makes a similar point: ". . . errors and foibles . . . occur every now and then in almost everyone's spontaneous speech. It is rather the massing and aggregating of these oddities and errors which characterize the communication [in schizophrenic families] (p. 149)."

When interaction processes are grounded within a "difficult" communicational field they may "get nowhere" and produce a sense of frustration and dissatisfaction on the part of system members. The situation is similar to that facing persons trying to maintain a conversation within the setting of a noisy room. Not only do the communicational fields that envelop interactors vary in difficulty, but system members differ in their ability to adapt, to deal with or to cope with "difficult" communications. Some persons are more vulnerable, for example, to negative or destructive communications, or less capable of meeting excessive demands. Such vulnerability can be due to differential thresholds for the perception of attacks or demands or to an inability to neutralize them.

This phenomenon is, perhaps, analogous to an organism's ability to process and neutralize noxious substances to which it has been exposed. Just as organisms can neutralize only small amounts of poisons encountered at infrequent intervals, so some persons are able to cope with threats or to meet demands only when these threats or demands are received in small dosages, well spaced in time. Interaction process environments become pathogenic when

the level of difficulty they present or the demands inherent in interacting within them exceed the neutralizing or coping abilities of the
members of the system.

Bales (1953), perhaps the most serious student of social interaction process among behavioral scientists, asserts that interaction
systems are "in trouble" if, in the long run, positive reactions do not
outweigh negative reactions. A balance favoring positive behaviors
(acts of support, affirmation, agreement) is seen as the empowering
agent for a forward movement in social process. This positive/
negative dimension of human interchanges can, of course, be conceived of and measured in many ways.

As anticipated, we found that concordance ratios were
higher in control families than in "schizophrenic" families. Yet these
differences were not as substantial as clinical reports would lead one
to assume. But surprisingly, when the findings yielded by our family
interaction data were compared with data reported in studies of
other social contexts (for example, studies of therapy and discussion groups), a much more significant finding emerged. Family contexts as a whole, whether or not they involve families with a mentally ill member, exhibit lower concordance ratios than any other
form of social context on which we had data available. Moreover,
family interaction process, as mirrored in the findings yielded by
our research, does not meet the criteria set forth by Bales for a
viable, task-oriented system. Twelve of the eighteen families studied
(under admittedly nonrepresentative conditions) exhibited a concordance ratio of less than 1.00. The family interactional environment then must be considered as a difficult context for interaction
—an observation that is, needless to say, not inconsistent with common experience.

When individuals with low thresholds to interactional demands, who are deficient in "neutralizing" capabilities, are exposed
to environments high in communicational difficulty, the likelihood
is increased that they will either tend to withdraw from the context
or to succumb to the formation of symptoms that make them likely
to become psychiatric patients. Such persons should, and indeed do,
manifest diminished symptomatic behavior when they are removed
from the family context and placed in social environments that are

differently constituted. Unfortunately, such contexts are often hospital or clinic settings, contexts not traditionally notable for ease of interaction. These locations are often accidentally rather than rationally organized. The developmental histories of a wide variety of so-called therapeutic contexts attest to this.

If, indeed, variations in environmental difficulties (conceived in relation to prevalence, balance, and spacing of "difficult" communication) are crucial, then more attention must be directed to the construction of social settings that take account of these requirements. These would be settings in which patients are exposed to a context of communicational acts and expectations that do not exceed their tolerance thresholds and do not tax them beyond their ability to neutralize frustrating and discordant communication. In such settings, communications would be balanced and the obstacles to interactional flow (disagreement and so on) present in other settings would be reduced. In our view, one effect of psychoactive agents is to increase thresholds for processing demands and noxious human stimuli. Unfortunately, their use helps to preserve existing dysfunctional environments, and to reduce the pressure toward the creation of environments with more suitable communicational structures.

ENHANCEMENT OF GROWTH AND DEVELOPMENT

Interpersonal relationships and interaction process patterns may be static or repetitive or they may be dynamic and progressive. Repetitive interactions, in the popular idiom, "do not go anywhere"; neither the relationship between the participants nor the interactional process seems to evolve. Such systems then do not exhibit expected phases of growth and differentiation.

Interaction contexts in which there is no interactional development or evolution may be deemed harmful, while those that provide the experience of participating in an evolving relationship or interactive process may be deemed beneficial or therapeutic. The development and programming of interaction does not necessarily require the collaboration of all system members but potentially can be stimulated by one system member alone. For example, a skilled parent helps a child to move through interactive phases and a skilled therapist does much the same for a patient.

In our studies and review of the literature, we noted that social systems with a schizophrenic member show little progression and interactive development. For example, families with schizophrenic members have been described as rigid. In such families behavioral differentiation, for example, that is required by changes in age status is avoided in favor of repetitiveness and stability.

In our work on therapy systems involving schizophrenic patients, we noted little differentiation in the allocation of behaviors over both shorter and longer time intervals. A therapeutic interaction context, then, would be one that exhibited phase differentiation and evolution and would encourage growth and development among those who participated within it; but it is an intriguing question as to whether one is actually able to find the appropriate interactive arrangement that would be capable of eliciting appropriate phase behavior from interactors irrespective of their psychological state and previous interactional history.

SYSTEM PROPERTIES OF INTERACTION PROCESSES

In this book we have undertaken to view the interaction process as a context. Like Bales, we believe that an interaction process exhibits system properties. We postulate that to the extent that such properties fully emerge in an ongoing interaction process, the effect of such interaction processes upon its contributors will be beneficial for members or functional for the system. We postulate that to the extent that these properties fail to emerge and operate, an interactional context will be harmful or dysfunctional.

PERMEABLE BOUNDARIES

The definition of a system requires a determination of what is inside and what is outside. Boundaries define this difference. Biological and social units are considered to be "open systems"; though their boundaries can be identified (for example, cellular boundaries, or membranes; social boundaries, or normative definitions of group membership), information and energy is diffused through such boundaries. System boundaries may be rigid or impermeable, in which case they become barriers between the system and the outside, or systems may have such thin boundaries that they have hardly any insulation from external forces and requirements.

Contexts that provide intact permeable boundaries that allow essential transactions to occur across them would appear to be those most optimally suited for the emergence of beneficial interaction processes within them. Some social systems, particularly the family system, can be conceived of both as a whole system with boundaries around it and a differentiated system within which subsystems (individuals, sets of role partners such as mother-child, father-mother, and so on) have boundaries that define a variety of limited intrapersonal and interactive processes.

Both Ackerman (1961) and Wynne (1958) suggest that disturbed families are "too well differentiated" from the outside world and that their boundaries are inappropriately rigid. Interaction process in such families fails to serve adaptive functions for the family members when they function in the non-family world, because normative and value information emanating from social surroundings are neither properly processed nor utilized within the family system. At the same time, a number of other students of the disturbed family, such as Bell (1962) and Bettelheim and Sylvester (1960), have suggested that such families suffer from "ill-defined and loose boundaries" and that the impact of the outside world has an overwhelming and disorganizing impact upon the occurrence of orderly transactions within them.

Our data on interaction patterns in families with schizophrenic youngsters support both of these clinical observations. For example, we found that dyadic subsystems in such disturbed families are especially averse to permitting interactional intrusion and redirection of interaction. We observed how, in such families, some subsystems (for example, mother-son dyad) would resist, for a sizable number of interactions, entry by another family member into the interaction subsystem. These findings certainly suggest that such interaction subsystems are rigidly bounded and impermeable to other interactors.

However, when we shift our attention from the dyad to individuals within such families, family systems with schizophrenic members exhibit deficiencies with respect to the individual's psychological boundaries. In our study of labeling communication we found that members of "schizophrenic" families continue to label, monitor, and effect to control experiential and feeling processes within other family members. Family members literally "invade" each other's inner space and the boundaries of such "inner space" become diffuse.

We consider social contexts to be enhancing in which spatial, physical, and psychological boundaries are respected. Traditional psychotherapy contexts usually meet this standard, but not always nor in all respects. For example, while labeling and monitoring interactions may be required in some phases of therapy interactions, as in some phases of familial socialization, at other phases they become dysfunctional. Boundaries are also violated in some other so-called therapy systems in the name of therapy (especially in state hospitals), and in such systems labeling and evaluative communications tend to be over-represented in the flow of interaction.

In our view, only those systems (whether familial, therapeutic, or educational) in which interactive or interpersonal boundaries are respected, however permeable, can give rise to interaction processes in which self-initiated and autonomous behavior is encouraged and enhanced.

HOMEOSTASIS AND EQUILIBRIUM

Fully developed and viable social systems exhibit tendencies toward equilibrium (homeostasis). Homeostatic processes refer to an ensemble of regulations that maintain variables constant and direct an organism toward a goal. Interaction process is the means through which social systems achieve homeostasis. A variety of types, patterns, and sequences of interactions are involved in maintaining equilibrium.

In order for an "open" social system to survive, it must be capable of maintaining its interactional parameters within limits that are defined both by the requirements of the system and the requirements of the larger systems of which it is a part. The maintenance of interactional parameters within such limits is accomplished by adjustments within the system, and homeostasis is achieved. The range of permissible deviation from the homeostatic norms of a system varies from system to system and from parameter to parameter. Homeostasis in social systems implies stability of behavior and expectations on the part of its members, but it may be crucial to ascertain how much and what kind of *instability* a system can tolerate before homeostatic constraints are brought into play. It is equally important to recognize that *invariability* or rigidity is an indicator of defective homeostasis; we have referred to this rigidity as pseudo-homeostasis, stability through nonadjustment.

Such equilibrium processes occur in relation to each major functional task that a social system performs. It is therefore possible for a system to exhibit self-regulatory processes in relation to some system functions and tasks, and fail to achieve homeostatic balance in relation to others. For example, we observe that "disturbed" families allow much less variability along certain dimensions than nondisturbed families. They are not able to tolerate the new level or array of behaviors on the part of family members that restoration of equilibrium requires.

In an adequately functioning social system the kinds and amounts of interactions required are generated from the participants as and when needed in the life of the social system. An obvious example here would be that while physical performances restore equilibrium early in the life of a mother-child dyad, verbal actions serve the same regulatory function later.

Information exchange and socialization (role induction) are among the major functional tasks that social systems accomplish through human interaction. Information exchange permits participants in social systems to orient themselves to both the human and nonhuman environments. Socialization results from the achievement of expectational and behavioral congruence in persons in the same social field.

When, for example, there is a lack of understanding and of complementarity of behavioral requirements in a functioning social system, information and instructions regarding appropriate expectations and behaviors are generated. But we observed that such self-regulative processes fail to occur in therapy systems involving a schizophrenic patient. The interaction process in such systems is deficient in compensatory primary system role information.

Systems in which homeostatic mechanisms cannot operate freely are likely to give rise to interaction patterns that impair the functioning of individuals that participated in them.

EXTRASYSTEM INPUTS AND ADAPTATION

Social systems represent solutions to larger problems posed by society. The interactional arrangements and processes within these systems represent implementations of these solutions. Being "open systems," social systems are constantly subject to extrasystem inputs, influences, and forces. Continuous adjustments and adaptations in interactional patterning within a social system are required to accommodate to this diversity of external influences impinging upon it.

The extrasystem inputs of most interest to us are norms, values, rules; in other words, the instructions issued to a social system and its members regarding intrasystem allocation of behaviors and patterning of performances—for example, with respect to the family system, the traditional instructions on the behavior and performances required of males and females, of young and old, of parents and children.

Special problems arise when such instructions are too diverse or not congruent with each other, especially when the instructions provided to different members of the system are insufficiently articulated and not compatible with each other. Lack of complementarity in behavior often reflects disparities in the sets of instructions provided. The adaptation problem might be reduced if instructions on how to resolve incompatible demands were to be issued with such demands. However, this is frequently not the case. Problems are created for a system when its members have to adapt interactionally to mutually contradictory or poorly integrated normative value requirements.

The imbalance of negative over positive interactions in family contexts and its harmful effects on more vulnerable members represent an example of such a failure in system processes. The family is a central arena for enacting and resolving instructions issuing from the normative and value structure of the wider community or the subsystem of the community within which the family is located. The structural and interactional arrangements within a family constitute adaptations to the tasks and demands of the cultural system. In our view, the demand structure of the cultural system contributes generally to the precarious imbalances that favor conflictual interactions in the family. For example, if parents are instructed to induct children into performances that are anachronous or are incongruent with the child's biological proclivities, conflict is inevitable. When adaptive functions are defective, intergenerational problems ensue. Overconformity, overcompliance, and oversensitivity to socialization requirements make the "teaching" generation persevere in the exercise of control behavior. This manifests itself communicationally in an excess of negative sanctions, disconfirmation, and the use of a variety of interpersonal restraining devices, including sarcasm and irony.

In addition to the conflicts surrounding age-status demands, are those centering around the male-female axis. Here instructions not only are received from a variety of sources, but are rapidly shifting and are differentially processed by each family member. The result is the development of a family pattern of differential expectations that are ill-articulated and difficult to integrate. The normative instructions centering around the male-female axis are perhaps more incongruous than those associated with any other social status differences. The family is the social context, however, within which these have to be enacted and resolved. No wonder, then, that it is so vulnerable to adaptational failures.

Family and psychotherapy systems are distinguished from most other social systems and organizations in that their task is not only socialization of their members to their own requirements, but also to help their members to interact appropriately and effectively in other social systems and the society at large. Both family and therapy systems are especially vulnerable to "adaptational" failure, but theoretically, at least, therapeutic socializers are supposed to bring more expertise to this task than are family socializers.

Some family systems reduce internal conflict by inducting members into a "closed" family system, and remain impervious to external demands. This very often takes the form of what Wynne (1958) refers to as *pseudo-mutuality*. Strain is avoided if stable arrangements can be worked out within the family, even though they might be dysfunctional and inappropriate for family members' adaptation in other social systems. For example, by not requiring changes in age-appropriate behaviors, communicational struggles can be avoided. However, persons "not acting their age" may have serious problems getting along in social and work relationships outside their family.

When family systems become overburdened by excessive extrasystem demands, adaptational failures ensue. Such failures are reflected in the imbalanced interactive arrangements that we referred to as pathogenic in the previous section.

DEUTERO-LEARNING

Learning is an almost inevitable accompaniment of human interaction. Moreover, learning may proceed on a number of levels while the process of interaction unfolds. The higher the order of learning that an interaction context makes possible, the more enabling and valuable the experience is for the participant.

On the simplest level, interaction provides concrete information about the interactors themselves as undifferentiated person-objects. The focus is upon behaviors or performances that are associated *with* the other rather than upon learning *about* others. The prototype of this learning is exemplified by an infant's relationship to a nurturing mother. It appears to us that perhaps interaction contexts that generate personality systems destined to be labeled as "psychotic" do not facilitate learning beyond this level.

The next level at which learning may occur through inter-action involves a first order of generalization. Persons, then, learn not only about specific others but also about behaviors character-istic of categories of others. They learn to identify categories of be-haviors that are characteristic of status or position (mothers, fa-thers, teachers). Experiencing interaction in a "normally" evolving social system results in the emergence of the role concept. As a result of interacting with another, one learns not only about him, but also about the category of others who hold similar statuses and positions in similar systems. Interaction then provides information about what behaviors characterize a class of persons. During interaction, information is acquired about the substantive contents and bound-aries of role relationships. For example, in a classroom context, one learns that teachers teach and that students are negatively sanc-tioned for not listening. Models of such interactive arrangements can then be used to generalize to other interaction settings that approximate the teacher-student paradigm.

In our discussions of the family and therapy contexts we indicated what aspects of interactive contexts and characteristics of system might contribute to the learning of the role concept and to the generalization of role behavior. For example, family systems in which interactional subsystems are aborted or atrophied inter-fere with the emergence of differentiated role conceptions and be-haviors.

Clinical observers have from time to time come upon the significance of subsystem development in interactive contexts to which they allude in the metaphor of their trade, but hardly in the dialect of our role or system conception. Consider, for example, the following interchange among clinicians at the Sea Island confer-ences on schizophrenia (Whitaker, 1958):

WARKENTIN: Does it seem to you that a schizophrenic could develop in a family where the father is the kind of person who insists on physical intercourse with his wife?

ROSEN: Where the husband and father insists on inter-course with the wife, do you mean?

WARKENTIN: Yes, you see, I don't believe that it is possible for schizophrenia to develop in such a situation.

ROSEN: I never heard of such a thing!

JACKSON: . . . we are saying that the sexual relationship is one of the ways in which the family dynamics are revealed . . .

Translated into a role behavior vocabulary, this interchange implies that "schizophrenic families" constitute undifferentiated system contexts in which different role relationships and positions do not entitle members to differential rights, performances, and demands. A child exposed to such an interactional context is not adequately exposed to differentiated role structures nor subsystem determinants of behavior. If all members of the primary system behave alike to all other members, then different behaviors do not become associated with different classes of persons and system positions. To conceive of all relationships as alike and undifferentiated in interactional form and expression is dysfunctional for later participation in systems other than the original family context. On the other hand, if interactional environments are *differentiated,* then one learns that the general class, "persons," is differentiated into subclasses of persons (men, women, parents, therapists, and so on). This learning can be utilized in interaction in other social systems where persons in these categories are present.

Besides an interactional environment being differentiated into role relationship subsystems, interaction patterns occurring *within* a role relationship can also manifest varying degrees of differentiation. We would argue that the possibilities for generalization are further enhanced if interactional patterning within a role relationship are well differentiated.

This is the import of Kaiser's (1965) criticism of the structure of the traditional analytic role relationship model of analyst and patient. If the conception of the therapy relationship were broadened into a more symmetrical, interactive one, the members would have more opportunity "to develop new ways of dealing with such problems as domination, submission, decision-making, liking and disliking, etc." (p. xxi).

Perhaps the highest order of abstraction about role learning that may occur during interaction is that which can be referred to by a term like *deutero-role-learning*. The concept of deutero-learning itself was introduced by Bateson (1942), who put it this way:

> It is a commonplace that the experimental subject—whether animal or man, becomes a better subject after repeated experiments. He not only learns to salivate at the appropriate moment, or to recite the appropriate nonsense syllables; he also, in some ways, *learns to learn*. He not only solves the problems set him by the experimenter, where each solving is a piece of simple learning; but, more than this, he becomes more and more skilled in the solving of problems . . . we might say that the subject is learning to orient himself to certain types of contexts, or is acquiring "insight" into the contexts and sequences of one type rather than another, a habit of "punctuating" the stream of events to give repetitions of a certain type of meaningful sequence.

Deutero-role-learning then would refer to "learning to learn role relationships." Individuals in one interactive setting learn to identify those rules and principles underlying the interactional patterning that enable them, when interacting in a novel context, to engage in a procedure of scanning the relevant array of known interactional fields to help them to learn the pattern of interaction prevailing in a new setting.

One can illustrate the notion of deutero-learning by reference to the learning of a card game. Learning a card game "prepares one for the learning of the next because one has not only learned the rules of the particular game, but also that card games involve—among other things—the distribution of cards among players, symbolic meaning of action, patterns of play, different values of cards, the use of strategy and deception," and so on (Lennard and Bernstein, 1960).

Deutero-role-learning may involve the learning of rules regarding the allocation of behavior, the establishment of intimacy, the generality of demand structures, and the nature of interactional cues that follow fulfillment and nonfulfillment of such demands.

Since interactional environments are specialized, they differ in the kinds of deutero-role-learning possible within them. Interaction processes in some family contexts fail to facilitate deutero-role-learning. Members of such families experience difficulty in new and different interactional environments. One of the significant functions of interaction contexts, which we would consider to be therapeutic, is to provide adequate opportunity for deutero-role-learning.

It appears to us that a number of properties of interaction process encourage and facilitate the occurrence of deutero-role-learning. The first condition is that the interaction process be genuine or authentic, and fully actualized. This means that the entire range of interactional potentials (both quantitative and qualitative) must be realized in the interaction. Social contexts in which there are too few verbal and behavioral interchanges do not lend themselves to deutero-role-learning. Incongruent and deceptive interactional behaviors also interfere with such learning. Thus therapeutic social contexts, when they tend to facilitate a maximum realization of interaction, accordingly, facilitate deutero-role-learning.

A second condition is fulfilled in settings in which interaction and interactors attend to the vicissitudes of the interaction process itself. In truly therapeutic contexts, attention is frequently centered on the existential state of the interaction process. The procedural and process difficulties that stand in the way of the development of complementarity between other actors are attended to and explored, and hopefully solved. The interactors are "system sensitive."

A third and last condition to be discussed here involves the "as if" or "playful" quality of interactional proceedings. Deutero-role-learning is encouraged when different interactional behaviors "can be tried on for size" and interactors can, without final commitment, investigate the implications and challenge the normative rules and principles that underlie behavior. The application of many of these ideas to modifications in psychotherapeutic techniques is explored in a recent book by Nelson, Nelson, Sherman, and Strean (1968).

INTERACTION AS END IN ITSELF

Of course, individuals must be motivated to interact or else none of these purposes can be accomplished. The salience of motives having to do with assuring the physical survival of the individual and the species is obvious and they need not occupy us overmuch here. It would appear that infants are *compelled* to interact with mothers or mother surrogates. Through interaction, they discover that release from physical tension (for example, hunger and thirst) can be obtained through contact with another person and her resources.

The absolutely essential role that interaction plays in "normal" development is not a modern discovery, as shown by a quotation from Salimbene, describing the unlooked-for side effects of an experiment conducted in the thirteenth century by Frederick II:

> . . . He wanted to find out what kind of speech and what manner of speech children would have when they grew up if they spoke to no one beforehand. So he bade foster mothers and nurses to suckle the children, to bathe and wash them, but in no way to prattle with them, or to speak the Hebrew language, which was the oldest, or Greek, or Arabic, or perhaps the language of their parents, of whom they had been born. But he labored in vain because the children all died. For they could not live without the petting and joyful faces and loving words of their foster mothers . . . (Stone and Church, 1957, p. 63)."

Yet, even beyond interaction in the service of survival and protection, human beings are characterized by their strivings for and dependence on interaction with other human beings. *Interaction becomes an end itself.* Most adults require contact with other humans in order to preserve their physical continuity and identity. It is this phenomenon that makes "solitary confinement" and being "placed in Coventry" such painful experiences. Interactional deprivation leads to anguish, loneliness, and depression. Interaction seems to serve functions that are essential to all of us. Though most individuals appear to exhibit an active need to interact, some individuals such as psychotics and hermits often do not.

On the most general level, there is evidence of a human requirement for minimum inputs to the various sensory modalities of sight, sound, and touch. Such inputs can, however, also be achieved through exposure to nature and person surrogates (mass media).

More relevant perhaps is the function served by interaction in defining and affirming the "humanness" of the self. By being recognized socially and responded to by another, the recipient of interaction achieves membership in a class of persons similar to himself and thus acquires an identity.

In this connection, Bateson (Ruesch and Bateson, 1951) tells the story of a shipwrecked sailor on the Javanese coast who was defined by the natives as a "large white monkey of unknown species." Having been defined as something less than "human," the sailor could not enter into communication with his captors to revise their original premise. To paraphrase Bateson: unable to make himself understood and to become the object of interaction, the sailor may have begun to become as doubtful of his own humanity as were his captors. Goffman (1961) and Szasz (1961) suggest that the dehumanization of persons defined as insane proceeds in much the same way.

Beyond affirming the quality of "humanness," interaction also defines and redefines the self and roles among interactors. Interaction enhances and authenticates the "identity" assumed by an individual and facilitates his orientation *vis-à-vis* his interaction alters. In this way, interaction reinforces paradigms of self-other relationships that have been postulated to be operating as "internalized I-Thou patterns" within the psychic structure of an individual.

Descartes' famous dictum, *"Cogito ergo sum,"* therefore deserves a new and more sociological restatement: "I am responded to, therefore, I am (what I am)" is probably prior to "I think, therefore, I am."

Postscript

Beyond the
Interactional
Perspective

A major theme of this book has been that the structural and interactive arrangements characterizing a social system are real and significant aspects of human environments; that these arrangements exercise both facilitating and limiting influences upon interactional contents, trajectories, and sequences, which are outside the awareness and the control of the participants. Indeed, that to an extraordinary degree, social contexts determine the behavior of persons who constitute them.

If this view is to be taken seriously, and we believe it imperative that it be so taken, then a radical reexamination of the design of contemporary therapeutic and rehabilitative programs and procedures is long overdue.

The major trends now shaping the substantive efforts of mental health professionals can be traced to two events in modern history: the introduction of the contemporary conception of mental illness when Pinel created the paradigm of the mental hospital and the invention of modern two-person psychotherapy when Freud developed psychoanalysis.

In one form or other, in spite of considerable lip service to the contrary, even in contemporary group psychotherapy, family therapy, and community psychiatry, the operative focus of professional activities has revolved around attempts to change the behavior of individuals rather than situations, and the manipulation of psychological variables rather than social system and interactional variables.

Interventions have almost always been aimed at individuals rather than social systems or contexts. Thus group therapy often consists of treating individuals in groups rather than treating groups of individuals; family therapy often consists of treating individuals within the family rather than treating the family; so-called therapeutic milieus (including hospital settings) are often places in which therapy is done to individuals rather than contexts that are in themselves therapeutic; and the main push of community mental health programs has been to make more individual therapy or consultation available to members of the community rather than to deal with the social factors within that community.

We view social systems as organized in a hierarchy of subsystems, for example, dyads within the family, which is in turn part of a community subgroup, which is in turn responsive to a larger community; or dyads within a ward, which is in turn embedded in a hospital organization, which is in its turn influenced by a county, state, or governmental bureaucracy. Each subsystem is subject to extrasystem inputs from the larger social systems that make up its context. Many so-called therapeutic social systems, in order to meet these kinds of extrasystem demands, often develop interactional arrangements within them that are inimical to their professed therapeutic goals.

Therapeutic intervention may therefore sometimes have to consist of modifying contextual arrangements so as to change the character of the extrasystem inputs, acting upon the given subsystem in which behavioral change is desired. This shift in focus applies as accurately to the individual behavioral subsystem called a personality as it does to a group, a family, or a hospital. The unit chosen for analysis and intervention must, at the very least, be shifted from the interacting individual to the interactive context in which he is located.

The logical implications of the thoughts expressed here require that all significant environmental contexts be examined from this point of view, especially those that have been designated as therapeutic. We earlier specified some of the prerequisites of therapeutic interactive arrangements and systems. We contend that no context can be regarded as therapeutic, no matter what its stated aim, unless it meets these criteria. This perspective then introduces a new set of tasks for mental health professionals and community mental health specialists; namely, to influence structural processes and interactive arrangements in social contexts in such a way as to meet specified therapeutic criteria.

Shifting the direction of efforts and recognizing the relevant unit of intervention will not in itself solve the problem. For once the interactive *environment* is identified as the relevant and strategic unit for intervention, our attention then naturally shifts to the determinants of such interactive arrangements. For unless these determinants can be identified and their effects upon the patterning of interaction can be controlled, our efforts, however well-meaning, will surely be unsuccessful.

Consider this recent prescription for a therapeutic community. "The goal is to create a conflict-free, warm, encouraging, reassuring environment with a minimum of stress for the patients" (Pasamanick, Scarpitti, and Dinitz, 1967, p. 16).

Now, in considering this goal, one must question to what extent any social context that is as subservient to as many demands, that must operate with as many constraints, and that involves such a wide variety of role occupants with distinct loyalties as does a psychiatric or mental health facility, can in fact be reorganized in such a way as to maximize the interaction and system processes that would actualize these therapeutic prescriptions. Consider, for instance, some of the specific demands, constraints, and conditions within which most public psychiatric facilities are forced to operate.

City, county, and state legislative codes place many restraints upon the design of the social and physical environment in a public mental health facility—fire regulations may interdict the use of drapes and carpets or of installing cooking facilities for patients; health considerations, regarding sterile food handling, may prevent the granting of permission for the families of patients to cook for them; building codes may determine the color of walls, prohibit the hanging of pictures, and so on; licensing laws may limit the performances allowable to staff members and restrict the hiring of personnel; mental hygiene laws may determine who may be admitted and who may be discharged, and what kind of liberties may be granted to different categories of patients; budgetary limitations may determine sleeping arrangements and the degree of privacy available to patients, as well as the availability of staff, entertainment, and educational opportunities.

A number of constraints upon the pattern of interaction that occurs within traditional mental hygiene settings also emanate from various role definitions and role expectations of the existing mental health professions. The behaviors of staff members frequently are determined by professional obligations and loyalties to professional peer groups, theories of treatment, ethical codes, and professional associations. Ultimate responsibility for patient care is often considered to be a medical prerogative, irrespective of the particular patient's problems or the needs of the situation.

Various pressure groups, organizations, and the norms and demands of the wider community also exert influences upon what transpires within many mental health contexts. The community demands to be protected from "deviant" and "potentially dangerous" individuals. Various forms of socially inacceptable behavior such as drug use, homosexuality, promiscuity, and juvenile behavior must be "treated." Employees, no matter how ill-suited as therapeutic interactors, cannot be replaced or reassigned except for gross incompetence or malfeasance. In addition to all of these difficulties, institutional settings themselves give rise to what Wilensky (1967) has called "failure in organizational intelligence," that is, the suppression of information reflecting adversely upon the performance of a staff member or of a category of staff members.

Interactional configurations as they occur in a psychiatric facility represent tortured compromises among all of these aspirations, demands, conditions, and constraints; and such interactional configurations constitute the environmental field within which patients and staff perforce must interact. The cumulative impact of such extrasystem constraints and demands tends to reduce the likelihood that within traditional treatment settings the essential criteria postulated for truly therapeutic contexts can be met.

We have presented the view that therapeutic or damaging potentials often inhere in social contexts rather than in individuals; now going beyond the interactional perspective, we acknowledge that the adequacy or inadequacy of treatment environments is not independent of the larger contexts of which they are a part. A strategy that is directed only at altering the interactive arrangements prevailing within an existing system will be incomplete without simultaneously directing some effort at changing features of that system's larger context.

A proliferation of new mental health programs and blueprints for the expansion of treatment, prevention, and rehabilitation services is now occurring. Unfortunately, too many of the current and planned mental health activities and treatment efforts still do not depart significantly from the traditional model of the individual as the case. And even more unhappily, when new therapeutic efforts are undertaken they are too often embedded and encumbered in a vast web of dysfunctional and conflicting instructions and constraints.

However, a few so-called innovative efforts are actually deserving of the name. In these, the conception of a treatment environment does at least seem to involve implicit recognition of the problems created by system-within-system relationships, and there is an emergence of the rudiments of system-oriented solutions. We suspect that the environments created in these newer efforts will generate a more favorable atmosphere for the emergence of interactional patterns and system operations that we deem likely to be beneficial to the groups and to the individuals within them.

To develop a strategy for changing institutional structures that will favor the emergence of optimal interactional environments within them is a task of the highest priority for those concerned with bringing about therapeutic changes and increases in social learning. However, to propose the details of such a strategy is both beyond the scope of this postscript and not directly derivable from our present understanding of system relationships. But we can indicate some directions along which such efforts may fruitfully proceed.

We consider it advisable that therapeutic environments be set apart both physically and structurally from hospital and clinic settings, as is already the case with many halfway houses and special treatment centers (for drug users, alcoholics, and so on). Because such contexts need to be, insofar as is possible, *disencumbered* from the mass of dysfunctional and often incompatible instructions and constraints to which such contexts, when located within existing complex social structures, are inevitably subject. In this way, extrasystem inputs are minimized and the demands upon interactional arrangements to be adaptive to the larger environment are diminished, thus they can retain sensitivity to intrasystem processes and requirements. It is clearly less difficult for staff members to engage in interactions that are responsive to and that encourage self-initiated actions on the part of patients when their time and attention are not absorbed in responding to extrasystem demands (hospital administrative requirements, city, county, and state regulations, and so on).

One criterion for a therapeutic interactional environment is the degree to which it encourages autonomous behavior and self-definition of experience, feelings, and personal identity. Applying restrictive labels (sick, deviant, delinquent) to system members inhibits the expression of autonomous behavior and transgresses—in a symbolic sense—the boundaries of system members. We favor social contexts that allow boundaries between subsystems to remain intact and sufficiently permeable so as to permit essential transactions to occur across them. Though labeling procedures are often inevitably involved in the process of social interaction, they tend to deprive persons and groups of options to vary their behavioral contributions and to freeze them into overspecialized and inflexible roles and statuses (patients, delinquents, troublemakers, paranoids, and so on). The very act of labeling tends to create excessively rigid and impermeable social system boundaries. The existence within a system of such boundaries reduces the system's potential for change and adjustment and interferes with the full realization of its system properties. Persons who are ordinarily the subjects for therapeutic processing often come already overencumbered and overburdened with the effects of persistent and lifelong labeling and monitoring.

One strategy we propose to restore viability and therapeutic potential to so-called therapeutic environments is to liberate them from the consequences of dysfunctional labeling procedures. *Unlabeling* is already implicit in many new therapeutic and rehabilitative programs in which the diagnosis of psychological deviance or symptomatology is postponed or downgraded and in those where legal and social sanctions against violations of rules and social deviance are temporarily withheld.

Suspension of labeling, or active unlabeling, increases the scope of autonomous behavior of system members and respects subsystem boundaries. But whether one can implement a commitment to intervention and change, without identifying the target of one's efforts, and thereby unintentionally assign persons to a career of deviant behavior, is not an easy question to answer.

The pattern of staffing in some of the newly created therapeutic settings has seen considerable changes. Sometimes these changes have occurred as a matter of choice, but more often because of necessity. Shortages in professional personnel, coupled with a commitment to reach a broader population base, have led to a greater utilization of paraprofessionals and indigenous personnel. Such *deprofessionalization* is evidenced in a number of programs, especially those located physically and philosophically apart from traditional medical and clinical facilities.

A structural change in the members composing a therapy system has direct implications for the interactional arrangements that may prevail within it. Professional specialization and its accompanying "settling" of commitments often lead to restrictions on necessary intrasystem inputs in an ongoing interaction system. An over-commitment to a particular theory of behavior and to the nature of one's professional task may limit a specialized professional from engaging in the whole range of interactional behaviors that are required for the maintenance of homeostasis or from contributing to the reduction of communicational stress and concordance, because it narrows the range and scope of his participation in the interactional field.

Many mental health professionals still try to remain loyal to a relationship paradigm that stresses asymmetry even when they have become uncomfortable with it. This relationship model appears to us to be dysfunctional for the actualization of the full range of interactional behavior necessary for deutero-learning to occur. Persons who are less well trained may be less constrained and hence more able to exhibit the full range of appropriate actions, reactions, and feelings required in a therapeutic interaction system. Accordingly, we believe that the trend toward deprofessionalization that is already under way in mental health settings should be encouraged.

We have earlier called attention to the untoward consequences of mystification when it occurs in the family context. But mystification is a process that is immanent in many social contexts. We are interested especially in the role that mystification plays in so-called therapeutic social contexts. When mystification occurs in such contexts it may be because of one or all of the following reasons. Information may be intentionally withheld or distorted, allegedly for the sake of the patient. Information may be withheld or falsified for structural reasons to protect one group of professionals or staff or the organization at large. Or, information may not be disclosed because information-giving is not a sufficiently salient feature of the role conceptions held by therapeutic personnel.

Providing less than the minimum level of information that is required for the socialization and orientation of members of a therapeutic system tends to lower complementarity of expectations, to impede role induction and to generally increase system strain. When staff or patients respond to such an informational deficit by seeking *disclosure* of the information that they require for system maintenance and their efforts are frustrated, the so-called therapeutic context becomes increasingly pathogenic.

Since mystification and the suppression of information can be functional as well as dysfunctional for social systems, efforts to increase the amount of disclosure and the amount of information available to system members may encounter considerable resistance. Several practical suggestions as to how this problem can be approached come to mind. Therapeutic personnel should be made aware of the therapeutic value of disclosure and demystification and should receive training in information giving. But it may also be necessary to create new and specialized positions within therapeutic settings that specialize in information collection, transmission, and disclosure. Access to such information specialists would guarantee that essential information would be available for purposes of induction, orientation, and demystification.

Another way to enlarge the array of information available, especially about the special work and the problems of other system members and the nature of the system as whole, could be accomplished through various system members temporarily exchanging places. Physicians who have been unfortunate enough to have occupied the patient role in a hospital setting can attest to the insights about patients and the hospital setting thereby gained.

The recognition by some researchers and theorists, during the past two decades, of the role of the family context in the development of individual deviance and disturbance, and as a unit for treatment and intervention, was a step in the direction of understanding the relation of context to individual behavior. But, paradoxically enough, though it led to a downgrading in the importance attached to the individual, in favor of the family, some workers tended to treat the family as if it existed in isolation, much as psychologists had tended to view individuals. Few social systems exist in isolation, and the family is not among them. Our theoretical position requires that attention always be paid to the effects of the larger social environment, in addition to a consideration of the effects of the particular context that is the focus of attention.

Our argument now needs to be addressed to those who,

having correctly moved their focus from the individual to the family context, are now proceeding to intervene without fully recognizing the family's vulnerability to prescriptions, demands, and values originating from outside its boundaries. Interactional configurations in families reflect and are sensitive to the values of the juvenile subculture via their adolescent children members, to definitions of human relationships supplied by mass media, and to an array of conflicting norms current in the community. To undertake, as some therapists do, to resolve the system strains within one family at a time, without taking into consideration the sources of these interactional strains, may be as limited in its way as the older focus on one family member at a time—a focus that family therapists reject with good reason.

We realize that this postscript goes beyond the interactional perspective originally proposed in this book. In accounting for individual variability and disturbance we had to shift attention from personality attributes to the effect of interactional environments. But, in considering how such environments and contexts, and the interaction processes that they comprise could be changed and modified, it became clear that any attack on existing structural and interactive social arrangements in families, wards, hospitals, or other significant social contexts also requires intervention in the larger social environment in which these contexts are embedded. Such extrasystem influences cannot be neglected if one wishes to render a social context more therapeutic. We have drawn attention to some of these extrasystem influences.

The critical question for the future is whether these influences are subject to modification. In this connection we are reminded of a phrase often quoted by Harry Stack Sullivan: "We must distinguish between the merely very difficult and the impossible."

References

ACKERMAN, N. Behavioral Trends and Disturbances of the Contemporary Family. In I. Galdston (Ed.), *The Family in Contemporary Society*. New York: International Universities Press, 1958, 52–69.

ACKERMAN, N. Preventive Implications of Family Research. In G. Caplan (Ed.), *Prevention of Mental Disorders in Children*. New York: Basic Books, 1961a, 142–167.

ACKERMAN, N. Unpublished memorandum, Jewish Family Service, 1961b.

ACKERMAN, N. Adolescent Problems: A Symptom of Family Disorder. *Family Process*, 1962, *1*, 202–213.

ALEXANDER, F., and FRENCH, T. M. *Psychoanalytic Therapy*. New York: Ronald Press, 1946.

BALES, R. F. *Interaction Process Analysis*. Cambridge, Mass.: Addison-Wesley, 1950.

BALES, R. F. The Equilibrium Problem in Small Groups. In T. Parsons, R. F. Bales, and E. A. Shils (Eds.), *Working Papers in the Theory of Action*. Glencoe, Ill.: Free Press, 1953, 111–161.

211

BALES, R. F. Preface to H. L. Lennard and A. Bernstein, *The Anatomy of Psychotherapy.* New York: Columbia University Press, 1960.

BARKER, R. *The Stream of Behavior.* New York: Appleton-Century-Crofts, 1963.

BARTON, A. H., and LAZARSFELD, P. F. Some Functions of Qualitative Analysis in Social Research. In S. M. Lipset and N. J. Smelser, *Sociology: The Progress of a Decade.* Englewood Cliffs, N.J.: Prentice-Hall, 1961.

BATESON, G. Social Planning and the Concept of Deutero-Learning. *Science, Philosophy, and Religion.* Second Symposium 2, 1942, 81–97.

BATESON, G. Cultural Problems Posed by a Study of Schizophrenic Processes. In A. Auerbach (Ed.), *Schizophrenia: An Integrated Approach.* New York: Ronald Press, 1959, 125–146.

BATESON, G., et al. Toward a Theory of Schizophrenia. *Behavioral Science,* 1956, *1,* 251–264.

BELL, N. Extended Family Relations of Disturbed and Well Families. *Family Process.* 1962, *1,* 176–188.

BERTALANFFY, L. VON. General System Theory and Psychiatry. In S. Arieti (Ed.), *American Handbook of Psychiatry,* Volume 3. New York: Basic Books, 1966, 705–721.

BETTELHEIM, B. *New York Times Magazine.* Jan. 12, 1967.

BETTELHEIM, B., and SYLVESTER, E. Parental Occupations and Children's Symptoms. In N. Bell and E. Vogel (Eds.), *The Family.* Glencoe, Ill.: Free Press, 1960, 499–509.

BIRDWHISTLE, R. L. *Introduction to Kinesics.* Louisville, Ky.: University of Louisville, 1952.

BIRDWHISTLE, R. L. Critical Moments in the Psychiatric Interview. Presented at the Galesburg State Research Hospital Tenth Anniversary Symposium, Oct. 22, 1960.

BOWEN, M. Family Relationships in Schizophrenia. In A. Auerbach (Ed.), *Schizophrenia: An Integrated Approach.* New York: Ronald Press, 1959, 147–178.

BOWEN, M. Family Concept of Schizophrenia. In D. D. Jackson (Ed.), *Etiology of Schizophrenia.* New York: Basic Books, 1960, 346–372.

BRIM, O. G., JR., and WHEELER, S. *Socialization After Childhood.* New York: Wiley, 1966.

BRUCH, H. Falsification of Bodily Needs and Body Concept in Schizophrenia. *Archives of General Psychiatry,* 1962a, *6,* 18–24.

BRUCH, H. Eating Disorders. *Special Treatment Situations.* Des Plaines, Ill.: Forest Hospital Foundation, Oct. 1, 1962b.

BUBER, M. William Alanson White Memorial Lectures, Fourth Series. *Psychiatry,* 1957, *20,* 97–129.

CHAPPLE, E. D. Quantitative Analysis of the Interaction of Individuals. *Proceedings of the National Academy of Science,* 1939, *25,* 58–67.

CHAPPLE, E. D., and ARENSBERG, C. M. Measuring Human Relations: An Introduction to the Study of the Interaction of Individuals. *Genetic Psychological Monographs,* 1940, *22,* 3–147.

CHAPPLE, E. D., *et al.* Interaction Chronograph Method for Analysis of Differences Between Schizophrenics and Controls. *Archives of General Psychiatry,* 1960, *3,* 160–167.

EMERSON, A. E. Discussion of *Homeostasis Reconsidered* by A. Rapaport. In R. M. Grinker (Ed.), *Toward a Unified Theory of Human Behavior.* New York: Basic Books, 1960, 225–246.

ENELOW, N., and ADLER, L. Foreword to L. Fierman, *Effective Psychotherapy: The Contribution of Hellmuth Kaiser.* New York: Free Press, 1965.

EPSTEIN, N., and WESTLEY, W. Patterns of Intra-Familial Communication. *Psychiatric Research Reports,* 1959, *11,* 1–9.

FESTINGER, L. *A Theory of Cognitive Dissonance.* Evanston, Ill.: Row Peterson, 1957.

FLECK, S., *et al.* Some Aspects of Communication in Families of Schizophrenic Patients. Paper read at American Psychiatric Association Meeting, Philadelphia, 1959.

FLEMING, J., and BENEDEK, T. *Psychoanalytic Supervision.* New York: Grune and Stratton, 1966.

FRANK, J. *Persuasion and Healing.* Baltimore: Johns Hopkins Press, 1961.

FREUD, S. Further Recommendations in the Technique of Psychoanalysis, 1913. In E. Jones (Ed.), *Sigmund Freud: Collected Papers,* Volume 2. London: Hogarth, 1949.

FREUD, S. Psychoanalytical Notes upon an Autobiographical Account of a Case of Paranoia, 1911. In E. Jones (Ed.), *Sigmund Freud: Collected Papers,* Volume 3. New York: Basic Books, 1959.

FROMM-REICHMAN, F. *Psychoanalysis and Psychotherapy: Selected Papers of Frieda Fromm-Reichman.* D. M. Bullard (Ed.) Chicago: University of Chicago Press, 1959.

GENET, J. *The Balcony.* New York: Grove Press, 1960.

GLOVER, E. *The Technique of Psycho-Analysis.* New York: International Universities Press, 1955.

GOFFMAN, E. *The Presentation of Self in Everyday Life.* New York: Doubleday, 1959.

GOFFMAN, E. *Asylums.* New York: Doubleday, 1961.

GOLDFARB, W., *et al.* Parental Perplexity and Childhood Confusion. In

A. H. Esman, *New Frontiers in Child Guidance*. New York: International Universities Press, 1958.

GOULDNER, A. W. Explorations in Applied Social Science. In A. W. Gouldner and S. M. Miller (Eds.), *Applied Sociology*. New York: Free Press, 1965.

HALEY, J. An Interactional Description of Schizophrenia. *Psychiatry*, 1959a, *22*, 321–332.

HALEY, J. The Family of the Schizophrenic: A Model System. *Journal of Nervous and Mental Disease*, 1959b, *129*, 357–374.

HALEY, J. Family Experiments: A New Type of Experimentation. *Family Process*, 1962, *1*, 265–293.

HARE, A. P. Review of H. L. Lennard and A. Bernstein, *Anatomy of Psychotherapy*. *American Sociological Review*, 1961, *26*, 288.

HOCH, P. H. Research: Ongoing and Needed. In S. C. Scher and H. R. Davis (Eds.), *The Out-Patient Treatment of Schizophrenia*. New York: Grune and Stratton, 1960, 203–211.

HOMANS, G. C. *The Human Group*. New York: Harcourt, Brace, 1950.

JACKSON, D. D. Family Interaction, Family Homeostasis, and Some Implications for Conjoint Family Psychotherapy. In J. H. Masserman (Ed.), *Individual and Family Dynamics*. New York: Grune and Stratton, 1959, 122–141.

JACKSON, D. D. The Study of the Family, unpublished paper which appeared in part as The Study of the Family. *Family Process*, 1965, *4*, 1–20.

JACKSON, D. D. Aspects of Conjoint Family Therapy. In G. H. Zuk and I. Boszormenyi-Nagy (Eds.), *Family Therapy and Disturbed Families*. Palo Alto, Calif.: Science and Behavior Books, 1967, 28–40.

JUNG, C. G. *Contributions to Analytical Psychology*. London: 1928. Quoted by M. McLuhan, *Understanding Media: The Extensions of Man*. New York: New American Library, 1966.

KAISER, H. *Effective Psychotherapy*. New York: Free Press, 1965.

KAPLAN, A. *The Conduct of Inquiry*. San Francisco: Chandler, 1964.

KOESTLER, A. *Darkness at Noon*. New York: New American Library, 1961.

LAING, R. D. *The Divided Self: A Study of Sanity and Madness*. London: Tavistock Press, 1960.

LAING, R. D. *The Self and Others*. London: Tavistock Press, 1962.

LAING, R. D. Mystification, Confusion, and Conflict. In I. Boszormenyi-Nagy and J. L. Framo (Eds.), *Intensive Family Therapy*. New York: Harper, 1965.

LAZARSFELD, P., and BARTON, A. H. Qualitative Measurement in the Social Sciences: Classification, Typologies, and Indices. In D.

Lerner and H. D. Lasswell (Eds.), *The Policy Sciences*. Stanford, Calif.: Stanford University Press, 1951, 155–192.

LENNARD, H. L. Analysis of Family Conflict. In N. Ackerman *et al.* (Eds.), *Exploring the Base for Family Therapy*. New York: Family Service Society, 1961, 145–150.

LENNARD, H. L., BEAULIEU, M., and EMBREY, N. G. Interactions in Families with a Schizophrenic Child. *Archives of General Psychiatry*, 1965, *12*, 166–183.

LENNARD, H. L., and BERNSTEIN, A. *The Anatomy of Psychotherapy*. New York: Columbia University Press, 1960.

LENNARD, H. L., and BERNSTEIN, A. Role Learning in Psychotherapy. *Psychotherapy*, 1967, *4*, 1–6.

LIDZ, T. The Relevance of Family Studies to Psychoanalytic Theory. Paper presented at the New York State Divisional Meeting of the American Psychiatric Association, New York City, 1961.

LIDZ, T. *The Family and Human Adaptation*. New York: International Universities Press, 1963.

LIDZ, T., and FLECK, S. Schizophrenic Human Integration and the Role of the Family. In D. D. Jackson (Ed.), *Etiology of Schizophrenia*. New York: Basic Books, 1960, 323–345.

LONGABAUGH, R., ELDRED, S. H., BELL, N. W., and SHERMAN, L. J. The Interactional World of the Chronic Schizophrenic Patient. *Psychiatry*, 1966, *29*, 78–99.

MATARAZZO, J. D. Prescribed Behavior Therapy: Suggestions from Interview Research. In A. Bachrach (Ed.), *Experimental Foundations of Clinical Psychology*. New York: Basic Books, 1962, 471–509.

MCLUHAN, M. *Understanding Media: The Extensions of Man*. New York: New American Library, 1966.

MEAD, G. H. *Mind, Self and Society*. Chicago: University of Chicago Press, 1934.

MERTON, R. K. *Social Theory and Social Structure*. Glencoe, Ill.: Free Press, 1957.

METRAUX, R., and HOYT, N. S. German National Character: A Study of German Self-Images, *Studies in Contemporary Cultures—B*. New York: American Museum of Natural History, 1953.

MEYERS, D. I., and GOLDFARB, W. Studies of Perplexity in Mothers of Schizophrenic Children. *American Journal of Orthopsychiatry*, 1961, *31*, 551–564.

MILLER, D. R. The Study of Social Relationships: Situation, Identity, and Social Interaction. In S. Koch (Ed.), *Psychology: A Study of a Science*, Volume 5. New York: McGraw-Hill, 1963, 639–737.

MILLS, C. W. Methodological Consequences of the Sociology of Knowledge. In I. L. Horowitz (Ed.), *Power, Politics and People: The Collected Essays of C. Wright Mills*. New York: Ballantine Books, 1963, 453–468.

MITSCHERLICH, A. *Auf dem Weg zur Vaterlosen Gesellschaft*. Munich: R. Piper, 1963.

MORRIS, J. N. *Uses of Epidemiology*. Edinburgh: Livingstone, 1957.

MURRAY, H. A. Toward a Classification of Interaction. In T. Parsons and E. A. Shils (Eds.), *Toward a General Theory of Action*. Cambridge, Mass.: Harvard University Press, 1951, 434–464.

NELSON, B. The Psychoanalyst as Mediator and Double Agent: An Overview. In M. C. Nelson *et al.*, *Roles and Paradigms in Psychotherapy*. New York: Grune and Stratton, 1968, 1–10.

NELSON, M. C., NELSON, B., SHERMAN, M. H., and STREAN, H. S. *Roles and Paradigms in Psychotherapy*. New York: Grune and Stratton, 1968.

NEWCOMB, T. M. An Approach to the Study of Communicative Acts. *Psychological Review*, 1953, *60*, 393–404.

NEWCOMB, T. M. *The Acquaintance Process*. New York: Holt, 1961.

OGDEN, C. K., and RICHARDS, I. A. *The Meaning of Meaning*. New York: Harcourt, Brace, 1938.

PARKER, B. *My Language is Me*. New York: Basic Books, 1962.

PARSONS, T. *The Social System*. Glencoe, Ill.: Free Press, 1951.

PARSONS, T. The Social System: A General Theory of Action. In R. R. Grinker (Ed.), *Toward a Unified Theory of Human Behavior*. New York: Basic Books, 1956, 55–69.

PARSONS, T., and BALES, R. F. *Family Socialization and Interaction Process*. Glencoe, Ill.: Free Press, 1955.

PARSONS, T., BALES, R. F., and SHILS, E. *Working Papers in the Theory of Action*. Glencoe, Ill.: Free Press, 1953.

PASAMANICK, B., SCARPITTI, F. R., and DINITZ, S. *Schizophrenic in the Community*. New York: Appleton-Century-Crofts, 1967.

PEPINSKY, H. B., and KURST, T. O. Convergence: A Phenomenon in Counseling and in Psychotherapy. *American Psychologist*, 1964, *19*, 333–338.

PITTENGER, R. E., *et al. First Five Minutes: Sample of Microscopic Interview Analysis*. Ithaca, N.Y.: Paul Martineau, 1960.

RAUSCH, H. Interaction Sequences. *Journal of Abnormal and Social Psychology*, 1965, *2*, 487–499.

RUESCH, J. *Disturbed Communication*. New York: Norton, 1957.

RUESCH, J., and BATESON, G. *Communication: The Matrix of Psychiatry*. New York: Norton, 1951.

SEARLES, H. The Effort to Drive Another Person Crazy—An Element in the Aetiology and Psychotherapy of Schizophrenia. *British Journal of Medical Psychology,* 1959, *32,* 1–18.

SCHEFF, T. J. *Being Mentally Ill.* Chicago: Aldine, 1966.

SCHEFLEN, A. E. *Stream and Structure of Behavior: Context Analysis of a Psychotherapy Session.* Behavioral Studies Monograph No. 1, Eastern Pennsylvania Psychiatric Institute, 1965.

SHANDS, H. C. Psychoanalysis and the Twentieth Century Revolution in Psychiatry. In J. Marmor (Ed.), *Modern Psychoanalysis: New Directions and Perspectives.* New York: Basic Books, 1968.

SIEGEL, S. *Nonparametric Statistics for the Behavioral Sciences.* New York: McGraw-Hill, 1956.

SINGER, M. T. Family Transactions and Schizophrenia. *Excerpta Medica, International Congress Series,* No. 151, 1967, 147–164.

SKINNER, B. F. *The Behavior of Organisms.* New York: Appleton, 1938.

SPIEGEL, J. The Resolution of Role Conflict Within the Family. *Psychiatry,* 1957, *20,* 1–16.

STANTON, A. H., and SCHWARTZ, M. S. *The Mental Hospital.* New York: Basic Books, 1954.

STONE, L. J., and CHURCH, J. *Childhood and Adolescence.* New York: Random House, 1957.

STRODTBECK, F. Husband-Wife Interaction Over Revealed Differences. *American Sociological Review,* 1951, *16,* 468–473.

STRUPP, H. *Psychotherapists in Action.* New York: Grune and Stratton, 1960.

SZASZ, T. *The Myth of Mental Illness.* New York: Harper, 1961.

TALLAND, G. A. Task and Interaction Process: Some Characteristics of Therapeutic Group Discussion. In A. P. Hare, E. F. Borgatta, and R. F. Bales (Eds.), *Small Groups.* New York: Knopf, 1955, 457–463.

WALLERSTEIN, R. S. The Current State of Psychotherapy: Theory, Practice, Research. *Journal of the American Psychoanalytic Association,* 1966, *14,* 183–225. Citing K. M. Colby, *A Primer for Psychotherapists.* New York: Ronald Press, 1951.

WERNER, H. The Concept of Development from a Comparative and Organismic Point of View. In D. Harris (Ed.), *The Concept of Development.* Minneapolis, Minn.: University of Minnesota Press, 1957, 125–148.

WHITAKER, C. (Ed.) *Psychotherapy of Chronic Schizophrenic Patients.* Boston: Little, Brown, 1958.

WIGGINS, L. M. *Mathematical Models for the Interpretation of Attitude and Behavior Change: The Analysis of Multi-wave Panels.* Unpublished Ph.D. Dissertation, Columbia University, 1955.

WILENSKY, J. *Organizational Intelligence: Knowledge and Policy in Government and Industry.* New York: Basic Books, 1967.

WIRTH, L. Clinical Sociology. *American Journal of Sociology,* 1931, *37,* 49–66.

WYNNE, L., *et al.* Pseudo-Mutuality in the Family Relations of Schizophrenics. *Psychiatry,* 1958, *21,* 205–220.

WYNNE, L., and SINGER, M. Thought Disorder and Family Relations of Schizophrenics, Results and Implications. *Archives of General Psychiatry,* 1965, *12,* 201–212.

Index

A

ACKERMAN, N., 17, 61, 91, 93, 103, 120, 158, 188

Adaptation: in family, 17; and norms, 191–193; in social systems, 16, 17; in therapy, 17, 18

Agreement: and continuity (Table 2), 120; with content vs. presentation-of-self statements, 116; and disagreement in "schizophrenic" and control families (Table 3), 122; explicit agreement, 115; ratio of explicit agreements to explicit disagreements (Fig. 15), 124; theoretical significance of, 113

ALEXANDER, F., 22
ARENSBERG, C. M., 10
AUERBACH, A., 74

B

Balance, optimal, 90; required for interaction, 92

BALES, R. F., 10, 28, 34, 35, 47, 49, 50, 56, 69, 88, 89, 90, 91, 102, 113, 114, 115, 184, 187

BARKER, R., 55, 60
BARTON, A. H., 43, 168
BATESON, G., 43, 61, 74, 93, 102, 158, 196, 199
BELL, N., 188
BENEDEK, T., 23

the proposition as unit, 57; the statement as unit, 57; units in the analysis of family interaction data, 97

Unlabeling, 207

V

Variability: as a result of context, 32; as a result of demands, 33

Volume of communication in "schiz-ophrenic" and control families (Fig. 8), 98, 99

W

WALLERSTEIN, R. S., 23
WESTLEY, W., 99, 100
WHITAKER, C., 194
WIGGINS, L. M., 60
WILENSKY, J., 204
WYNNE, L., 53, 61, 91, 93, 114, 119, 120, 158, 184, 188, 193